On the Side of Liberty

A Unitarian Historical Miscellany

Alan Ruston

The Lindsey Press
London

Published by the Lindsey Press
on behalf of the General Assembly of Unitarian
and Free Christian Churches
Essex Hall, 1–6 Essex Street, London WC2R 3HY, UK

© General Assembly of Unitarian and Free Christian Churches 2016

ISBN 978-0-85319-087-5

Designed and typeset by Garth Stewart, London

Printed and bound in the United Kingdom by
Lightning Source, Milton Keynes

On the Side of Liberty: A Unitarian Historical Miscellany

This book is published by The Lindsey Press on behalf of the General Assembly of Unitarian and Free Christian Churches.

Unitarianism is a progressive religion whose historical roots lie in liberal Christianity. Its congregations have evolved over the past 350 years into diverse communities which draw on insights from many religious, philosophical, and scientific traditions. It emphasises the primacy of individual reason, conscience, and experience in matters of faith, and it is strongly committed to social action and human rights.

www.unitarian.org.uk

Contents

Introduction

When the Lindsey Press Panel invited me to prepare a selection of my published articles for a book about the story of Unitarianism, I realised that the project needed a theme. My publications have ranged widely in coverage, so, with the general reader rather than the historian in mind, I decided to choose 'Unitarian people' as the central theme. It has been people with all their vagaries of character and activity that have chiefly interested me, rather than ideas and theology.

The field is a rich one, as Unitarians tend to have strong characters and they have achieved much – or at least these are the attributes of those about whom I have written. My output (and there has been a great deal of it) began in the 1960s and continues into the present. The first piece included here was published in 1967, and the last piece in this volume appeared in 2013. My full historical bibliography appears in the *Transactions of the Unitarian Historical Society* for 2015.

It has been necessary to edit each piece for this volume, as the style of presentation has varied over the years, and material written with historians in mind often needs amplification for the interested general reader. Sources have been included, but readers who wish to see the detailed references should consult the original article, the location of which is cited at the end of each extract. I have tried to eliminate overlap in content, but a certain degree of repetition is unavoidable, particularly in writing about nineteenth-century events. I hope that this selection constitutes an interesting and thought-provoking survey of some leading Unitarians, their achievements and varied characters, and that it will also provide insights into what others have thought about them in their own time.

Some definitions

The origins of Unitarian congregations, and even some of their ideas, need explanation, because certain of the terms used may be unfamiliar to general readers. Each has been written about extensively, and what follows is a very brief explanation to clarify the terms used; it is not intended to be exhaustive.

Arian

In early Christianity, disputes arose about the nature of the relationship of Jesus Christ with the Godhead. Some believed that Jesus could not be separated from the eternal God; others believed that he was supreme but not part of God by nature. Arians agreed that the existence of Christ pre-dated creation, but they argued that it came later than the existence of God the Father. Although Christ was divine, his was a lesser kind of divinity than that of the Father, who was the Supreme Being. This view was expressed and led by Arius (an ascetic Christian priest in Alexandria, who died in 336) – hence the term *Arian*. The dispute was such that a Council of the Church was needed to resolve it; this took place at Nicaea in Anatolia (modern Turkey) in 325. There was ultimately a vote, and Arius lost. Out of this decision arose the concept of the Trinity, the tripartite God. Disputes continued, however, as Arian ideas have repeatedly reappeared at different times over the centuries. Opposition to the concept of the Trinity in the seventeenth and eighteenth centuries was expressed by individuals whose theology was Arian, and this proved to be a precursor to the Unitarianism that developed later in the eighteenth century.

The origins of British Unitarian congregations that have existed in the past two hundred years can be classified in the following three categories.

English Presbyterian

Ever since the Protestant Reformation in the sixteenth century there had been some individuals and groups who refused to conform to the established Church of England because they considered that it was either corrupt or insufficently evangelical. But modern English nonconformity dates from the restoration of Charles II in 1660 and the re-establishment of the Anglican Church of England and episcopacy after their abolition following the Civil War. The terms of the Restoration religious settlement were so severe that many ministers and their supporters refused to conform to the national Church. A large number of these ministers were consequently ejected from the Church of England in 1662 and eventually established Presbyterian congregations, seeking to create a simpler pattern of church life that was less reliant on what they saw as Catholic ritual. The other major denominations – the Independents (also called Congregationalists), the Baptists, and the Quakers – also rejected the idea of a national church and had already separated from the Church of England. The oldest nonconformist congregations were formed in this period of persecution, but most were founded after freedom of worship was allowed when James II issued his second Declaration of Indulgence in April 1687, a freedom confirmed under William and Mary by the passing of the Toleration Act in 1689.

By the late eighteenth century most Presbyterian congregations, including some in Wales, had been influenced by heterodox religious ideas, in particular the unitarian (i.e. non-trinitarian) thinking of Joseph Priestley, supported by his friend Theophilus Lindsey. By the early nineteenth century unitarian thought had spread widely, particularly among wealthy Presbyterian congregations, but many members remained Arian and even orthodox in their theology. Not all the congregations who adopted unitarian beliefs by the middle of the nineteenth century wished to drop the title Presbyterian, in part for legal reasons connected with the origins of their particular congregations. (The situation became more complicated after the founding of the Presbyterian Church of England in 1844, an association of the churches formed by Scottish Presbyterians in England.)

General Baptist

The core of Baptist belief centres on baptism, which its adherents hold should take place in adulthood, not during childhood; this view came to be expressed in certain small congregations in the first half of the seventeenth century. These early Baptists formed the General Baptist Assembly (GBA) in 1647. Later, the term 'General Baptist' was applied to those who believed that everyone was capable of being saved from damnation; the term 'Particular Baptist' identified those who affirmed that only an elect few would reach heaven. Following splits and disputes, the number of congregations continuing in membership of the GBA fell, and later in the eighteenth century those that remained, mainly in Surrey, Kent, and Sussex, began to adopt unitarian views. By the mid-nineteenth century most of the GBA member congregations had adopted a unitarian standpoint; an agreement between the British & Foreign Unitarian Association and the Baptist Union in 1915 identified those that were to be affiliated with the former, and those affiliated with the latter.

Protestant dissenter/Unitarian

In 1813, Parliament passed The Trinity Act (or more accurately 'An Act to Relieve Persons who Impugn the Doctrine of the Holy Trinity from Certain Penalties'). For the first time the holding of unitarian views became legal (and in this volume from this point onwards an upper-case initial letter will be used: *Unitarian*). Congregations formed after that date could describe themselves more precisely, rather than using the all-encompassing term 'protestant dissenters' which hitherto had been required.

It should be added that in this volume the words *dissenter* and *nonconformist* each appear with a lower-case initial letter, rather than a capital letter. The term 'dissenter' means 'dissenting from the Church of England'; it was in active use until the nineteenth century, when 'nonconformist' came to be widely accepted, meaning 'not conforming to the Church of England', and the older term fell out of general use.

Abbreviations

B&FUA

B&FUA stands for 'British and Foreign Unitarian Association'. A national organisation representing churches and congregations which avowed Unitarian beliefs did not exist before 1825, when the B&FUA was founded. It was not widely supported before the 1870s, and even then its Unitarian name in particular was contested. However, from then on it was more broadly accepted as the representative Unitarian body, both at home and abroad, until the foundation of the General Assembly of Unitarian and Free Christian Churches ('the GA') in 1928. The B&FUA became an incorporated body in 1915, to enable it to act as a continuing trustee of funds and churches, a role which it continues to perform among Unitarian churches today.

CL

The Christian Life: a weekly journal, assertively Unitarian in character, founded by Rev. Robert Spears in 1876, which presented a different view from that of *The Inquirer*. Spears continued to edit it until his death in 1899. In the twentieth century it lost its way in the changed religious environment and was assimilated into *The Inquirer* in 1929.

Essex Hall

The site in Essex Street, off the Strand, in central London where Rev. Theophilus Lindsey opened the first avowedly Unitarian chapel in 1774. After the congregation moved to Notting Hill Gate in the late 1880s, an office and meeting place were erected on the site, which continues to serve as the administrative office for the B&FUA and the GA. The building was destroyed by enemy action in 1944, and the present premises were erected on the original site in 1958.

GA

General Assembly of Unitarian and Free Christian Churches, formed in 1928 to fulfil many of the roles previously performed by the B&FUA and the National Conference. It operates its administrative functions from Essex Hall in London.

HMC

Harris Manchester College: the abbreviated version of the name 'Harris College and Manchester Academy', which succeeded Manchester College Oxford in 1996.

Inq

The Inquirer: the oldest dissenting newspaper still in existence, launched in July 1842. Until the early 1970s it was a weekly paper, since when it has appeared fortnightly. For longish periods during its history *The Inquirer* has been the only Unitarian journal. All extracts included in this volume are reprinted with permission.

MCO

Manchester College was founded at Cross Street Chapel Manchester in 1786 for the education of aspirant ministers, as well as lay people bound for the professions. The College migrated to York in 1803, then back to Manchester in 1840, and to London in 1853. It removed to Oxford in 1889 and the new buildings were opened there in October 1893. Run by its own Council, Manchester College Oxford ceased to exist when Harris College and Manchester Academy was formed by Royal Charter in 1996 as an integral College within the University of Oxford.

MR

Monthly Repository: the first openly Unitarian monthly journal, founded by Rev. Robert Aspland, which first appeared in January 1806. It was a pioneering intellectual journal of the early nineteenth century. Aspland passed the ownership and the editorship to Rev. W. J. Fox in the early 1830s, when it became a primarily literary journal. The *MR* ceased publication in December 1838.

National Conference
The National Conference of Unitarian, Liberal Christian, Free Christian, Presbyterian and other Non-Subscribing or Kindred Congregations was formed in the early 1880s by the B&FUA to provide a wider focus within the movement than the Unitarian Association could provide. It did this by holding Triennial Conferences, starting in 1882, and developing ministerial selection procedures. It was abolished with the foundation of the General Assembly in 1928.

Oxford DNB
Oxford Dictionary of National Biography. Key figures mentioned in this book shown with * against the first mention of their name have a biographical entry in the *Oxford DNB*. Copies of the book are held in most large libraries and universities, and an online version can be accessed from a personal computer or phone via most counties' on-line services by typing in the unique County Library number allotted to each reader.

TUHS
Transactions of the Unitarian Historical Society. The journal of the Unitarian Historical Society has appeared at least yearly since 1916. Collectively the Transactions constitute the major source of information about the history of Unitarianism in the UK. Numerous libraries in Britain and a few in the USA have long runs of the journal. All extracts included in this volume are reprinted with permission.

UCM
Unitarian College Manchester, founded in 1854 in Manchester as the Unitarian Home Missionary Board, with Rev. J. R. Beard as its first Principal. It became the Unitarian Home Missionary College in 1889, and the Unitarian College Manchester in 1926. The College owned its own premises from 1905 until 1985, when it relocated to Luther King House, becoming part of the Northern Federation for Training in Ministry (later the Partnership for Theological Education) within the University of Manchester.

Access to quoted sources

London is the place of publication of sources quoted or cited in this book, except where stated otherwise. The name of the publisher (where known) has been included for books published after 1990.

The sources cited or quoted in this book can be consulted at Dr Williams's Library, 14 Gordon Square, London, WC1H OAR (info@dwlib.co.uk) and at the Library, Harris Manchester College, Mansfield Road, Oxford, OX1 3TD (library@hmc.ox.ac.uk). Another comparable resource is Special Collections, John Rylands University Library of Manchester, 150 Deansgate, Manchester, M3 3EH (library.manchester.ac.uk/rylands).

Local Libraries and Record Offices hold material related to congregations and chapels in their area. Some of the published works quoted here are online, and www.unitarian.org.uk has a selection of them. Another route is www.unitarianhistory.org.uk, the website of the Unitarian Historical Society, which – besides including the text of certain articles – has a wide-ranging bibliography of published works concerning Unitarianism in Britain.

The
Eighteenth
Century

1 Being a dissenter in 1711

If you could go back and stand in the shoes of a dissenter from the Church of England in 1711, the date when the Unitarian Meeting House at Bury St Edmunds was built, it would seem like being in a different world. As L. P. Hartley wrote in *The Go-Between* (1953): 'The past is a foreign country; they do things differently there'.

Back then, the dissenters were basically still puritans, who were nastily described by G. K. Chesterton, in his biography of Bernard Shaw (1909, p. 43) in these terms:

> people who refused to contemplate God or goodness with anything
> lighter or milder than the most fierce concentration on the intellect.
> A Puritan originally meant a man whose mind had no holidays.
> To use his own favourite phrase, he would let no living thing come
> between him and his God; an attitude which involved eternal
> torture for him and a cruel contempt for others.

Chesterton (a Roman Catholic, incidentally) added, even more unfairly: 'it was better for the Puritan to worship in a barn than in a cathedral, for the specific and specified reason that the cathedral was beautiful'. There is more than a germ of truth in this, but Chesterton ignored or was unaware of the fact that for dissenters a barn or a house was in their early days the only place where they could meet.

Chesterton certainly would not have understood the simple and dignified beauty of the typical square and unadorned meeting house of the period, and the thought and understanding of the people who created it. These dissenters did not see how their relationship with their God and their community of worshippers could be expressed in anything but a simple structure built in the style of the Bury St Edmunds Meeting House, so unlike a cathedral or parish church.

Figure 1. The Unitarian Meeting House in
Churchgate Street, Bury St Edmunds, built in 1711
(Unitarian Historical Society)

To start with, it was called by dissenters 'a meeting house', which means literally a place where the faithful met together. 'Meeting house' has a very similar meaning to the word 'synagogue', taken from the Biblical term 'a place of gathering'. It was not a chapel, and certainly not a church. The meeting house was where members of the community met to pray and hear the Bible expounded. Those who gathered at Bury St Edmunds (hereafter Bury) were English Presbyterians, in 1711 still the largest group in numbers among dissenters, but their religious outlook was similar to other dissenters who also met in Bury. Both groups followed the writings and example of ***Richard Baxter** (1615–1691), a key leader of the Presbyterian/Independent cause who had died not many years before. Although they were called Presbyterian, there was no synod and certainly nothing like a synod in this part of England.

The dissenters in Bury in the main still associated freely with each other, and the difference between the groups was more a matter of emphasis than a major difference in principle or belief. By the late eighteenth century the situation had evolved into something different. The last time the minister of the Presbyterian-cum-Unitarian meeting house at Bury participated in an ordination service in the chapel of the other main dissenters (Independent, later Congregational) in the town was on 19 June 1800. 'Henceforth the doctrinal differences were too great to permit such friendly relations; the Presbyterian congregation at this time became distinctly Unitarian and the Independents no longer sympathised with them' (*Inquirer* 27 April 1889).

A minority under attack

In 1711 the dissenters were a beleaguered minority, although – since the Act of Settlement of 1689 following the accession of William and Mary to the throne – they were able to meet and erect their own meeting houses. It looked as if all would be well, but from 1710 the Sacheverell riots spread across England. These riots were led by rabble supporters of the Tories and were directed against dissenters, whom they accused of being of the Whig party, judging them to be 'monsters and vipers'. As David Wykes has pointed out (in *Persecution and Pluralism*), 'Dissenters locally were subject to verbal abuse, frequent petty acts of harassment, intimidation, even violence'. In particular there was strong feeling against those dissenters who also attended Church of England services occasionally in order to hold certain offices (in education, for example, in which sphere dissenters would supposedly speak vile things against the Church). An Act of 1711 forbade 'occasional conformity', but in most places the ban proved unenforceable, and the Act was repealed in 1719.

A Schism Bill was under discussion from 1710; many thought it would return dissenters to an almost outlawed status. It sought to create an Anglican monopoly in education. The resulting Schism Act 1714 was rarely enforced and was repealed in 1719. Persecution of dissenters was a regular occurrence, particularly at the time of public elections. The meeting house at Chester, for example, was nearly destroyed twice, and rioters burned down the one at Newcastle-under-Lyme in 1702. Fortunately things improved with the arrival of the Hanoverians in the shape of George I in 1714, and the assumption of political power by the Whigs. But in 1711 this agitation was at its height and anti-dissenter feeling was rumbling about. It was a brave act to open a new meeting house in that troubled year.

What were these people like, those who filled the new Bury building when it was opened on 30 December 1711? To start with, they were not Unitarian in belief, or even Arian, or probably anything like it. They were people of the Book, which was at the centre of their personal and family life, and many of their beliefs could be called neo-Calvinist (i.e. the beliefs of a convinced elect who believed that they were automatically saved from hell). They were Trinitarian, and it was not until the long ministry of William Lincolne between 1757 and 1792 that they became mainly Arian in belief, worshipping God the Father alone, seeing Jesus as subordinate but still divine. They placed great emphasis on the King James Version of the Bible of 1611, from which they quoted endlessly. The first avowed Unitarian minister to be appointed at Bury was **Dr Nathaniel Phillips** in 1801.

What were the services like then? There are few contemporaneous accounts available, but the pattern followed by *Matthew Henry, the Presbyterian minister at Chester, is seen as typical. The minister at Bury from 1690 was the similarly named *Samuel Bury (1663–1730), who studied at Doolittle's Academy in London for the training of congregational ministers, where Matthew Henry was a fellow student. Bury's exact theological views are not known, except that he refused to belong to a party or theological group, which makes commentators identify him as a liberal in his time. He claimed that he never prostituted himself to any party, but endeavoured to serve God as a catholic Christian (by which he did not mean Roman Catholic). Whatever his beliefs were, he was an energetic and successful preacher and minister.

Long services on a Sunday

Samuel Bury would have followed a similar pattern of working to Henry's at Chester.

Henry's constant work, on the Lord's-day at Chester, was to pray six times in public, to sing six times, to expound twice. He went to the congregation exactly at nine, began the public worship with singing the 100th psalm; then prayed, a short but fervent and suitable prayer, then he read some part of the Old Testament, and expounded it, going through it in course, from beginning to the end; then he sang another psalm, then he prayed for about half an hour, then preached about an hour, then prayed and sang and gave the blessing. He did exactly the same in the afternoon, only expounding the New Testament. This was his constant Lord-day's work.

(Bogue and Bennett, 1833, Chapter 5)

What a marathon: services lasting two hours or more, with 30 minutes of extempore prayer and about 20 minutes spent explaining a text. Preaching and prayer were undertaken without notes, as the spirit moved. It is not surprising that in some places someone was appointed with a long stick to wake people up. Box pews were not comfortable, without any cushions or padding. The congregation sat most of the time and were generally silent. Only psalms were sung: no hymns except on special occasions, and standing up to sing them was not universal. There was no music (it was a suspect activity in services); only a tuning fork might be used. Small orchestras to accompany the singing came later in the eighteenth century.

At the end of a Sunday the minister must have been exhausted, though perhaps his personal reward was that he was a figure of great power in his community. He spoke with real authority, not only from the pulpit but also in social gatherings. There were no evening services, and lighting the candelabra (where they existed) was a rare and quite costly event. Tallow candles were the cheapest form of light, but as they were made of animal fat, they smelt; wax candles were necessary, but they were expensive.

And what happened when the families – and all of them attended – got home? 'After retirement for the secret exercises of devotion, in reading and meditation, and prayer, the family was called together, the children and servants catechised and questioned on the discourses which they had heard, a sermon was read, and psalms were sung and the day was concluded with fervent and solemn prayer'(Bogue and Bennett).

Elizabeth Bury

Did what was done at Chester apply at Bury? The diary of Elizabeth Bury, the wife of the minister, shows a similar pattern. She died on 20 May 1720, aged 76, just after they had moved to Bristol on Samuel's appointment as the minister of Lewin's Mead Meeting House. Samuel edited her diary extensively, to present her always in a devout light; it was published as an aid to devotion, and she was presented as an exemplar. The book sold well. It was republished in 2010 by Gale ECCO in the USA. Unfortunately the original is lost, which would have revealed more of Elizabeth's true nature. Extracts demonstrate her concern about the servants' spiritual health, for she regularly quizzed them on the contents of the sermon. Similar devotions were held on most nights of the week. Not all families were as fervent as this, although most are likely to have had daily prayers morning and night.

Elizabeth Bury was a paragon of virtue, of whom the famous hymn writer Isaac Watts in a form of obituary said she was 'a pattern for the sex in ages as yet unborn'. A rich widow when she married Samuel in 1697, she was 19 years older than him. She got up at 4 am every day to pursue her studies in French, Hebrew, music, heraldry, mathematics, natural philosophy, anatomy, medicine, and divinity. She, like so many in the congregation, was no light dilettante.

Not only were there long Sunday services to attend, but also lectures in the week to go to, in the chapel and elsewhere, nearly all related to a Biblical theme. Elizabeth's diary records: '25 January 1699, I walked to a Lecture safely and without prejudice to my health, at 16 miles distance, and had entertainment to my Soul there.' And there were meetings for women: '6 December 1711, I was much revived at a meeting of good Women for Prayer and Repetition in which my heart was warmed.'

The congregation ignored Christmas and similar festivals, seeing them, like the regular repetition of the Lord's Prayer, as little more than Popish heresies. But they did listen to 'Fast Sermons' given by the minister. A Fast Sermon was not an exhortation to fast, but a discourse that was penitential in tone and was declared nationally to be given at times of crisis like war or famine. Samuel Bury reports of his late wife that 'she bore her part in

7

them with great fervency and zeal'. She seems to have been a paragon of dissenting virtue, and oh so serious.

One of the key services of the year, for dissenters in particular, was to celebrate the exposure of the Gunpowder Plot to blow up Parliament in November 1605. Long rousing sermons against Roman Catholicism were the norm on these occasions. The holding of a service of worship to celebrate Guy Fawkes Day on 5 November we would find odd, but dissenters and to a large extent the Church of England saw it as an occasion to give praise for what was presented as deliverance from Popery in England. Communion was held about once a month, generally after morning service; sometimes the congregation sat around a table, but more often they would serve each other as the plate and cup passed from hand to hand. The ceremony was simple but still could be a matter of much dispute.

Offshoots in the country

The Evans List of dissenting causes circa 1715, held at Dr Williams's Library in London, shows that there were 700 members at Bury – an amazing number. Obviously they could not all fit in a building that could house roughly 150 at most. Where were they from, and where did they meet? Some met in places within Bury, but other meetings were located in nearby villages. This happened in other places too. From the 1690s onwards there are registrations of places for public worship located in barns, private houses, and farms. These were outstations of the main congregation. Examples of scattered small worshipping groups in villages round the hub of a town meeting can be found all over England.

The minister's job was an onerous one, as he was expected to visit each sub-congregation at least once a month. The Ancient Chapel at Toxteth in Liverpool, for example, had 12 of these out-of-town congregations at about this time. Samuel Bury was paid well, at £80 a year; many Baptist ministers existed on less than £25. The sexton, in comparison, was paid £2 a year. With the help of his wife's money, Bury advanced cash for the erection of the building before all the subscriptions came in to meet the cost. He was not paid back in full until 1714.

The salary paid to Samuel Bury shows that the congregation was quite well off for a dissenting community; it consisted mainly of farmers, tradesmen, manufacturers, and the like. By 1711 there were few gentry, nor were the poor present in any numbers. Pew rents were the main source of income for the meeting house; sometimes they had sliding scales of payment. Nowhere outside London or the city congregations was it pitched at a high figure; between 10 shillings and £1.10 shillings per quarter was the norm.

There are few statistics to show the income levels of congregations at this time, but their ability to erect this meeting house in the centre of the town shows that its supporters had ample means. The town of Bury St Edmunds generally at this time attracted the well-to-do to live there. Margaret Spufford quotes a comparative study of this period, based on the official returns made of tax paid on household hearths. In counties in eastern England, Independents (later Congregationalists) and Quakers had on average 2.2 hearths per household and Baptists 1.9, but Presbyterians had 3.1 per household. They could afford to keep themselves relatively warm.

The ministers' power

Of course, not all members of the congregation behaved themselves as they should, and the minister acted with great power in this respect. The presbyter, as the minister was called, was said to be like a bishop in his own congregation. The Heads of Agreement among dissenting meetings of the 1690s stated: 'In the administration of church power, it belongs to the pastors and other elders of every particular church, if such there be, to rule and govern.' How was this governance exercised? There was no governing committee – that was a nineteenth-century invention – but there were groups of influential members, such as the trustees whom the minister consulted, and the pew holders who provided the regular income.

There were regular meetings of the members in some Presbyterian congregations to discuss internal issues. In such a closed group there were of course whispers and gossip, for the whole dissenting community of Bury, as in other towns, was small. All the dissenters were concerned about the reputation of the dissenting interest, as it was called, especially if the Church of England could make much of dissenters' transgressions, which they did if mishaps became known. The frisson of tension between dissent and the established Church was often found in small towns and rural areas until the early twentieth century.

Maintaining the health of the community, and ensuring that 'bad eggs' did not spoil it, was achieved by suspending (or at the most extreme expelling) members. This was called 'discipline', and some congregations kept a discipline book. It was quite a threat to be disowned by the community of which you and your family were so much a part. Presbyterians were among the first to abandon the practice of discipline, although books are to be found in Baptist congregations dating from the 1770s; there is an example recorded in the minute books at Framlingham Presbyterian Meeting House in 1774. By the start of the nineteenth century they had generally disappeared. To show the nature of these discipline cases, here is an example from a later period, taken from the Old Meeting House, Ditchling, Sussex, which was General Baptist. Similar examples will have existed in Presbyterian groups early in the century.

> *May 10th 1757 Church meeting. The case of John Vincent was considered and whereas he has been admonished several times and has promised a reformation, but still remains in a careless way and seldom goes to any hearing of a Sunday and follows gaming and keeping of bad company and breaks his promises in regard to making good his payments, therefore we agree to withdraw from him for such disorderly walking.*

The phrase 'disorderly walking' was commonly used among dissenters then, and we know exactly what it means. The Heads of Agreement of the 1690s, a form of national understanding among leaders of the dissenters, mention 'scandalous or offensive walking', which required offenders to be admonished or censured, generally in public, to seek their recovery from sin. Suspensions happened at Bury, as Elizabeth Bury's diary demonstrates:

1ˢᵗ July 1716. After Sermon, a Poor Penitential, after long suspension, was re-admitted to our communion with great seriousness and solemnity by the Pastor; and I hope true repentance in the offender. Lord! Let this awaken others who stay suspended.

The great divide

What was the nature of the social and religious divide between dissenters and members of the Church of England? The division was not necessarily between the ministers and the vicar or rector, with whom relations could be polite if not cordial; but it could be savage between lay members. In smallish towns like Bury with a strong dissenting interest, the split spread much wider between lay people than between ministers. Until the late nineteenth century, for example, shopkeepers who were dissenters attracted and expected the continued custom of their fellow dissenters. The same situation obtained for the Church of England. *William Hale White, writing as Mark Rutherford, based his novels (such as *Mark Rutherford's Deliverance*) on his dissenting youth in Cowfold (in reality Bedford), and he, like *Mrs Margaret Oliphant in *Chronicles of Carlingford*, describes the social position of nonconformists in the nineteenth century vis-à-vis members of the Church of England.

The two groups lived in almost different worlds, made even more separate by class distinctions. Unless it was essential, they often did not even speak to each other. Individual dissenters were badgered to conform and threatened with consequences if they did not. The Church of England regarded the consequences of the end of its religious monopoly as dire. High-churchmen refused to bury the children of dissenters, on the grounds that they were not properly baptised. This tendency became an organised activity in Derby in 1712, and it led the dissenters to create their own burial grounds.

It was for this reason that not meeting one's payments was considered to be a real sin. The dissenter was not only letting down his fellow dissenting tradesmen in financial terms but was also diminishing their whole community in the eyes of the Church of England. In the case of

John Vincent at Ditchling in 1757, failure to meet his payments is the final reason given for his suspension, but it was probably the significant one. A reputation for moral rectitude, honesty, and sobriety was important to maintain in small, often rural, communities.

Marriage generally took place between those associated with the same congregation. Wedding ceremonies up to the early 1720s took place in dissenting churches. The practice tended to disappear after this. In 1753 it was banned altogether outside the Church of England by Hardwick's Marriage Act. Marriage between a dissenter and a member of the Church of England was almost inconceivable within a small town. Dissenters who sometimes attended worship in the parish church were engaged in an activity that was more than frowned upon by most dissenters, although it was not unusual among the richer Presbyterians. Baptists who occasionally conformed by going to what they called 'the mass' were usually ejected from their community.

Ministers who came from dissenting academies were almost advised in their training to find rich widows among their congregations to marry; this is what Samuel Bury did: his wife, much older than he, was a widow left with ample means. A leading dissenting minister from a later period, *Job Orton (1717–1783), on advising a young man in a letter not to marry a penniless girl, wrote: 'you may reasonably expect, considering your education, profession and station, that you may meet with a wife with a handsome fortune, as many other dissenting ministers have done' (quoted in D. Coomer, 1946). Rich widows and heiresses were therefore much sought after by dissenting ministers, whose position made them attractive to serious-minded women.

Daily life of dissenters in 1711

How to sum up what life was like for a dissenter in 1711? It was a serious, devout life, bounded by the Bible and centred on the meeting house. There was much emphasis on the family: not only one's own immediate family but also that which gathered in the meeting house. You mixed with your own kind, the dissenting interest, and not outside it. Your dress was sober as you yourself were (with exceptions, of course, when it came to alcohol). The avid pursuit of money by an individual was frowned upon – although things in London, as ever, were rather different.

Apart from the upkeep of an unpretentious building and providing the minister with a moderate stipend, the group had few calls on their purses. There were generally small endowments, often involving gifts of land, which fulfilled most expenses from year to year. The congregations generally had a few poor members, such as labourers, and their particular needs were met from within the congregation. There were no central organisations to maintain, and trust funds to support the Presbyterian denomination were in the main established and supported by the wealthy London dissenters. Pew rents became payable once the building was completed, and they varied little from year to year; if the minister created a real upset for one reason or another, then these rents could decline and he could be forced to leave – but not really for any other reason, except for conforming to the Church of England.

While exciting things happened in the wider world, in a quiet country town like Bury St Edmunds the moral earnestness of the dissenter just continued in the same tenor from year to year. Membership of some meeting houses, particularly Presbyterian, did decline after 1715, however, as some richer members, not over-concerned with theology, found it easier all round to join the parish church. Later generations would conclude that the dissenters' life around 1711 was in the main a boring one, not only because of their strict views but also because dissenters were under attack and kept in their place by the Church of England system and the social mores of the time. Among dissenters, imagination was not seen as a desirable quality, and the primacy of the word meant that appeals to the emotions were downplayed. A few years later the hymns of *Isaac Watts helped to introduce an enhanced vision into the dissenting mentality. A notable verse from one of Watts's hymns expresses something brighter and less dour. Most dissenters of the early eighteenth century are likely to have judged this verse as an appropriate expression of their affirmations:

The voice that rolls the stars along
Speaks all the promises,
Where reason fails with all her powers,
There faith prevails, and love adores.

Sources

Bogue, D. and J. Bennett, 1833, *History of the Dissenters*.

Browne, B., 1877, *Congregationalism in Norfolk & Suffolk*.

Coomer, D., 1946, *English Dissent*, London.

Duncan, J., 'Samuel Bury', MS at Dr Williams's Library, London.

Macrae, F., c. 1946, *History of Ditchling Meeting House*.

Muller, J., 2007, *Cities Divided. Politics and Religion in English Provincial Towns 1660–1772*, Oxford University Press.

Nuttall, G. and O. Chadwick, 1962, *From Uniformity to Unity*.

Oxford Dictionary of National Biography.

Protestant Dissenters Magazine, 1794, Vol 1.

Routley, E., 1960, *English Religious Dissent*, Cambridge University Press.

Sell, A., 1990, *Journal of the United Reformed Church History Society*, May 1990.

Skeats, H. and D. Miall, 1891, *History of the Free Churches*.

Spufford, M., 1995, *The World of Rural Dissenters 1520–1725*, Cambridge University Press.

Strickland, G., 1730, *An Enquiry etc*.

Tong, W., 1721, *Account of the Life and Death of Mrs Elizabeth Bury died 1720*.

Wykes, D., 2006, *Persecution and Pluralism. Calvinists and Religious Minorities in Early Modern Europe 1550–1700*, Verlag Peter Lang.

This chapter is based on an address given at the Unitarian Meeting House, Bury St Edmunds, in 2011 to mark the 300th anniversary of the building; published online at www.ukunitarians.org.uk/pdfs/Being a Dissenter in 1711.

---

2 Price and Priestley at the Gravel Pit, Hackney

*Rev. Dr. Richard Price took up his appointment at the Gravel Pit Chapel as morning preacher in March 1770. He had become discouraged after nearly 14 years' ministry at Newington Green meeting house, because of the smallness of the congregation. Unwilling to sever his connections there completely, he continued as afternoon preacher. **Rev. Nathaniel White** (1730–1783) was appointed afternoon preacher at the Gravel Pit at the same time as Price and served until he left in 1774. White was followed in April 1775 as afternoon preacher by **Rev. William Metcalfe** (died 1790) of Kingston, who continued until Price became afternoon as well as morning preacher at the Gravel Pit in 1783.

Price's audience at Hackney was far greater than he had experienced at Newington Green, a fact which cured the despondency he was suffering from at the time. His arrival did not immediately increase the size of the congregation. 'During the first four or five years of his ministry, however, it increased very slowly; and it is possible that neither the excellence of his discourses, nor the impressive manner in which they were delivered, would have made any great addition to his hearers, had not other causes of a very different nature concurred to render him popular' (Morgan, p. 37).

'Notorious' is probably a better description of Price's reputation in the wider community. When the government proclaimed a Fast Day, an occasion when penitence was called for nationally, Price took the opportunity in sermons to put forward his views on the war in America. These made his name a household word, and he was widely lampooned and attacked in the press. His Sunday congregations at Hackney were often large, and the former sleepy nature of the Gravel Pit changed completely. But on Fast Days these congregations were even bigger, as the curious wished to hear Price, who was seen as afire with passion and zeal for liberty, justice, and peace. His two most important addresses were preached at Hackney and published in 1779 and 1781 respectively. Their force and fire reflected the sentiments of an increasingly radical congregation, who supported Price both in his public addresses and in his important works on population and mathematics (which included his ground-breaking work on the creation of life-expectancy assessments used by insurance companies).

Price attempted to live a quiet life with his wife (they had no children) in Newington Green. In 1787, following his wife's death, he moved with great reluctance to Hackney, to nearby St Thomas's Square. 'At this time indeed every exertion was painful to him, and he seemed to be almost as much oppressed by the dread of the trouble attending his removal, as by his sorrow at quitting a place where he had enjoyed so many hours of comfort and happiness' (Morgan, *op. cit.*).

Figure 2. 'Smelling Out a Rat; or the Atheistical-revolutionist Disturbed in his Midnight "Calculations"': James Gilray's caricature (1790) of Richard Price, haunted by a vision of Edmund Burke, the conservative political philosopher. Hanging on the wall is a depiction of the beheading of Charles I.
(Wikimedia Commons)

The congregation and Price's death

Few congregational records of this period survive, so all we can gather about the members is from lists of subscribers and from private letters and diaries. The account books show that a major alteration to the chapel building was made in 1787. Dr. Price's shorthand journal confirms the point:

> *July 15th 1787. This day sennight the subscribers met and agreed to shut up the meeting after the last Sunday in this month in order to enlarge it, but I think of this with some pain fearing that the generality reckon too much on the increase of the congregation and their continuing want of room.*

> *23rd September 1787. This day the meeting house was opened after being shut for enlargement seven Sundays. It is made about one third part larger and I heartily wish the interest may so prosper here as to continue to show that this was a necessary measure.*

The same source demonstrates that the congregation did expand during Price's tenure as minister:

> *November 18th 1787. My acceptableness as a minister is such as I hope makes me useful likewise in this capacity, the congregation here being almost doubled since I came to it.*

It appeared to be the rule at this time and into the following century for the treasurer to change yearly. Families like the Brooksbanks, Cottons, and Agaces continued their membership, but new faces and families appeared as Hackney increased in size. **Joseph Travers** could be considered a representative figure during this period. A sugar baker of Queen's Street, Cheapside, his name appears on most of the subscription lists. He had ten children, the second of whom, **Benjamin Travers FRS* (1783–1858), was the founder of modern eye surgery and was for a period a member of the congregation, having married a relation of Dr. Price.

There were many distinguished visitors to Dr. Price and his chapel from political and economic spheres. John Adams, ambassador to the

Court of St James 1785–1788 and later President of the USA, was an example. Writing to Price only a year after his return to the USA, he stated, 'There are few portions of my life that I recollect with more satisfaction than the hours I spent at Hackney, under your ministry, and in private society, and conversation with you in other places'.

According to *Joseph Priestley, 'During the last six years of his life, Dr Price confined himself to the morning service at Hackney, which he regularly performed until 20 February 1791 when he preached his last sermon (to mark his resignation). On 23 February he was taken ill of a slow nervous fever, occasioned by his attending the funeral of a friend at Bunhill Fields, and he died on 19 April 1791' (J. Priestley, *Discourse on the Death of Dr Price*, 1 May 1791). *The Gentleman's Magazine*, hardly a supporter of radical thinkers, in its obituary for Price (1791, p. 389) commented: 'Whenever history shall rise above the prejudice which may for a time darken her page, and celebrate the eras when men began to open their eyes, to behold their own rights, and when this gave rise to the splendid Revolutions of America and France, the name of Price will be mentioned among those of Franklin, Washington, Fayette and Paine.'

Through his intellect and ability, Price made a significant impact on the congregation. One of the few records from the period shows that he was largely instrumental in the founding of the Sunday School: on 31 January 1790 he took the chair at the inaugural meeting and was the first subscriber. Although he preached Arianism, it is clear that many of the congregation were individually Unitarian in belief, and his support for Lindsey's Unitarian Chapel in Essex Street in London in 1774 indicates that he was fostering Unitarian belief although not following it himself.

The arrival of Joseph Priestley

Dr. Priestley was the leading candidate to succeed his friend as a minister of the Gravel Pit congregation. A letter to Priestley, dated 7 November 1791, states: 'We the Committee of the congregation assembling at the Gravel Pit, have been deputised by a general meeting to invite you to accept the office of co-pastor to that society.' Priestley accepted in the following terms: 'After having been driven by violence, highly disgraceful to the Government under which we live, from a situation on every account most pleasing to me, I think myself happy and honoured by an invitation to succeed Dr Price' (Rutt, Vol. I). The violence to which Priestley referred was the burning down of the Birmingham meeting house of which he was the minister, earlier in 1791.

No reference is made in the letter to the background to the invitation, nor to the presence of Hackney College (for the training of ministers), which was an attraction to Priestley as it was to his predecessor. In 1790 Price hoped that his nephew *George Cadogan Morgan (1754–1798), who had filled the pulpit for a time, would succeed him. It was not to be, and the argument was over who should be the co-pastor with Priestley in 1793. Here the Hackney College connection was most important. *Rev. Thomas Belsham, a tutor at the College, wanted the job, but the influential Dr. Abraham Rees (1743–1825), also a tutor, did not support his colleague's candidature. The situation was made the more complicated by the College students, who were chapel members. They did not vote for Belsham, although they did not vote against him. In the end Rev. Michael Maurice (1766–1855) was elected by one vote; he was a former pupil of Rees, first at Hoxton and then at Hackney College. Chiefly Maurice is known as the father of *Rev. F. D. Maurice, the well-known Anglican theologian and Christian Socialist. Michael Maurice, who was an Arian, had only a short tenure of office at Hackney.

*William Morgan (1750–1833), brother of George Cadogan Morgan, welcomed Priestley into his home – at some cost to himself, as his guest was so widely disliked for his political views that he was unwelcome elsewhere in the area. Priestley determined to take a long lease on a house in nearby Clapton, and 'the first few months of his residence at Clapton were uneventful, though it could scarcely be said he was welcome there. Shopkeepers, women and servants shunned the Priestleys and their home. It was difficult to find people to work for them in any capacity' (Gibbs, p. 184 *et passim*).

His life was made tolerable because of his friends: *Gilbert Wakefield (1756–1801), for example, who lived nearby, was a Unitarian difficult to fit into any category, although he was certainly connected with the congregation. In his autobiography Priestley states: 'On the whole, I spent my time even more happily at Hackney than I ever had done before; having every advantage for my philosophical and theological studies, in some respects superior to what I had enjoyed at Birmingham, especially for my easy access to Dr Lindsey and my frequent intercourse with Mr Belsham.'

Priestley commenced his ministry at the Gravel Pit in December 1791; the account book shows that he was paid 10 guineas for his activity during that month. He followed his usual ministerial pattern: 'In this situation I found myself as happy as I had been at Birmingham; and contrary to general expectation, I opened my lectures to young persons with great success, being attended by many from London; and though I lost some of the hearers, I left the congregation in a better situation than that in which I found it' *(Autobiography)*. With such a contentious figure as minister, it could hardly be otherwise. The subscription of £105 raised for him after he had left for America shows some key names in the congregation missing from the list as contributors. Times were harsh, and in February 1794 he heeded the urgings of his friends to leave as soon as he could, lest he be arraigned by the government before the courts for insurrection. He booked passages for himself and his wife, and sailed on 8 April 1794. He preached his farewell sermon at the Gravel Pit on 30 March to a large congregation. Many Unitarians, it must be said, breathed a sigh of relief at his departure. One of them wrote to *The Gentleman's Magazine* in September 1793: 'Dr Priestley has represented the Unitarians as a body of men so devoid of respect for the government of this country, as to conceive kings, lords and commons to be no better than a gang of rascals and highwaymen.'

Sources

Cone, C. B., 1952, *Torchbearer of Freedom*, University of Kentucky Press.

Dissenters Magazine, May 1899.

Gibbs, F. W., 1965, *Joseph Priestley*.

Green, E. H., 1913, *A Short History of the New Gravel Pit Sunday School*.

Maurice, F. (ed.,) 1884, *Life of F. D. Maurice*.

H. McLachlan, *TUHS*, 1925.

Morgan, W., 1815, *Memoirs of the Life of Rev Richard Price*.

Priestley, J., 1791, *A Discourse on the Occasion of the Death of Dr Price*, delivered at Hackney 1 May 1791.

Rutt, J. T. (ed.), 1817–31, reprinted in 1972, *The Theological and Miscellaneous Works of Joseph Priestley*, London.

Rutt, J. T. and A. Wainewright, 1792, *Memoirs of the Life of Gilbert Wakefield*.

Thomas, B., *Richard Price's Journal, 1787–1791*.

Thomas, D. O., 1979, *Price/Priestley Newsletter*.

Thomas, R., 1924, *Richard Price*, Oxford.

Wilson, W., 1808, *Dissenting Churches in London*.

This chapter is based on part of Chapter 3, 'The Revolutionary Period', in *Unitarianism and Early Presbyterianism in Hackney*, by Alan Ruston, privately published, 1980.

3 Two Unitarians in France during the Revolution

'The most sensible women', wrote the poet *George Dyer in 1792, 'are the most uniformly on the side of liberty; witness a Macaulay, a Wollstonecraft, a Barbauld, a Jebb, a Williams, and a Smith.' *Mary Wollstonecraft is today the best-known name, but none knew as much of the French Revolution at first hand, had such opportunities to observe it closely, and left so complete a record of what she saw, heard, and thought as *Helen Maria Williams. There is no full biography of her, although references to her writing and activity are found in many published works on the period. Her connection, though slight, with the poet *William Wordsworth, is perhaps best known. His first poem appeared in the *European Magazine* of March 1787: a sonnet entitled 'On seeing Miss Helen Maria Williams weep at a Tale of Distress'. Throughout his life Wordsworth held a high opinion of Helen and her writings, although even in her own lifetime she was already being forgotten.

However, other people had a different opinion of her and her books. In the 1790s she was a hated figure in England and was widely lampooned and attacked in the press. She lived in France from 1792. Two factors fuelled English detestation of her: her open liaison in Paris with *John Hurford Stone, who besides being a divorcé was an assertive and advanced Unitarian; and her constant avowal of liberty in all things, particularly in religion. Their connection with Joseph Priestley and the publication of a correspondence with him in America made both of them among the most disliked English people living abroad. Stone might well have been convicted of treason and hanged had he returned to England after 1794. This chapter is a sketch of their lives, their Unitarian connections, and their contribution to the later development of radical religious thought in France.

Helen Maria Williams was born in London on 17 June 1761, the daughter of Charles Williams of Aberconway, an officer in the army and of Huguenot descent. Her mother, Helen Williams (1732–1812), née Hay, of Naughton in Scotland, came of an old Protestant family. Following the death of Charles in 1769, the family moved to Berwick-on-Tweed, which was where the young Helen grew up. A precocious child, she was writing verse at an early age, her mother being her sole instructor. In 1781 Helen came to London with her poem 'Edwin and Elfrida', a legendary tale in verse, which aroused the interest of *Rev. Dr. Andrew Kippis, who wrote an introduction to it and found a publisher for it. It was well received, and from then on Dr. Kippis' protegée maintained an output of poetry – sentimental, melancholic, and humanitarian – sufficient to ensure her popularity. An 'Ode on the Peace' in 1783 was followed in the next year by 'Peru', a rather more ambitious complaint against the European exploitation of South America. Her growing fame won her the patronage of the influential George Hardinge, who encouraged her literary efforts, assisted the 1786 publication of her 'Poems', and contributed materially to their success. In 1788 she returned to the theme of Peru with 'A Poem on the Bill Lately Passed for Regulating the Slave Trade'.

She was undoubtedly greatly influenced by Kippis, and her growth into Unitarian belief clearly dates from this period. 'It was Kippis who inspired her with her first religious ideas. From then on she frequented the company of the Dissenters' (Woodward, 1930). At his death in 1795 she wrote:

Him through this lengthening scene I mark with pride
My earliest teacher and my constant guide.
First, in the house of prayer, his voice impress'd
Celestial precepts on my infant breast;
The hope that rests above, my childhood taught,
And lifted first to God my ductile thought.
(*Gentleman's Magazine*, January 1796, p. 66)

The young *Samuel Rogers, the poet, was friendly with her. The only letter that has been preserved (14 November 1787) from Dr. Kippis to Rogers states that 'Miss Helen Williams desires his company at tea on Monday next. She lives at Mr. Jacques's, the first house in Southampton Row, Bloomsbury, opposite Russell Street.' Rogers spoke of her in later years as a fascinating person, though not handsome, and he became intimate with her in this early period of his life. It is from these literary and religious connections that she developed a passion – her enemies called it a madness – for liberty, whether on behalf of the enslaved negroes or the oppressed Greeks (Clayden, 1887, p.77).

The lure of France

With sentiments like these, the lure of France at the time of the Revolution was considerable. From the beginning of 1789 Helen and her sister Cecilia (there was also another sister, Persis) had been taking French lessons from their friend the Baroness du Fossé. In 1790, Baron du Fossé, who later wrote several Unitarian works and had recently succeeded to an estate in France, invited the sisters to visit him. Following Cecilia, Helen landed in France on 13 July 1790, thrilled by the spectacle of 'France standing on the top of golden hours' (Todd, 1948). She returned to England in the September completely converted to the principles of the Revolution. She had already written to a friend in England: 'And I, too, although a foreigner in the land of happiness, add my voice to this universal concert and cry with all my heart, "Vive, vive la Nation!".' In 1791 Helen persuaded her mother and two sisters to return with her to France, after publishing 'A Farewell for Two Years to England', in which she announced her intention of sojourning 'Where the slow Loire on borders ever gay Delights to linger, in his sunny way'.

Figure 3. 'Ardent for liberty': Helen Maria Williams (1761–1827) (Wikimedia Commons)

They were well settled in the Rue de Lille in Paris before the attack on the Tuilleries on 10 August 1792, which marked an important stage in the French Revolution. Her writing of these events with enthusiasm, passion, and lack of reserve brought many in England to dislike what Helen appeared to represent. After the massacres of September 1792, the Williams family took an apartment in the Rue Helvetius (ten years later she moved to the Quai Malaquai), and here she settled down – never, so far as is known, to return to England. She established her own salon, at which she was hostess every Sunday evening to the principal Girondists (a faction within the French Assembly advocating war to spread the revolution). Helen soon became well known, too, among the English in Paris. At the banquet of Englishmen in the White Hotel, Paris, on 18 November 1792, with John Hurford Stone in the chair, to celebrate the French victories, toasts were drunk: 'To the speedy abolition of hereditary titles and feudal distinctions in England, the coming Convention of Great Britain and Ireland, and the lady defenders of the Revolution, particularly *Mrs Charlotte Smith, Miss Williams* and *Mrs. Barbauld.*' Each had strong radical dissenting connections. The dinner and the toasts were widely reported in the British press.

Helen sealed her fate in English eyes with the publication of the third and fourth volumes of her *Letters from France* in 1795/96, dealing with the events of 1793/94. Of the third volume, however, only the first letter was her own composition; six were written by John Stone. The final letter was by *Thomas Christie (1761–1796), the Scottish revolutionary enthusiast, who had similar religious connections. Every word seemed calculated to set English teeth on edge, because written from the standpoint of the other side.

By this time Helen and John were living together. Both had been imprisoned in Paris during 1793, and he again in 1794. M. Ray Adams (1939) sees their coming together in the following terms: 'They were made to understand each other. Both were generous in their feelings and ardent for liberty. Why they kept the exact nature of their relationship secret it is hard to say. It has been thought that Bishop Gregoire secretly married them after John Stone had announced his divorce from Rachel Coope in June 1794.' Certainly their relationship was an open secret, and they were lampooned by their critics in England. One wrote a poem entitled 'The Union of Liberty':

> Then came Helen Maria Williams Stone
> Sitting on a goat with bearded chin;
> And she hath written volumes many a one;
> Better the idle jade had learned to spin—
> Dearly she loves a philanthropic sin,
> Called fornication — and doth it commit;
> Nor Careth she for modesty a pin,
> And laughs at Satan and the burning pit;
> Ah! dame! be like one day you'll know the truth of this.
> (*The Anti-Jacobin Review*, 1801)

An article in *The Anti-Jacobin* for the same year made a similar point: 'What! because she, Helen Maria Williams, has thought fit to renounce her native country as *too moral* for her propensities, to live avowedly to the world with the *husband* of her friend'.

John Hurford Stone

John Hurford Stone played a significant role in Helen Williams's life and at the Sunday salons. He was born on 19 December 1763 at Tiverton, lost his father in childhood, and was sent to London with his brother William to assist in the business of their uncle, William Hurford, the son of a Tiverton sergemaker, who had become a coal merchant. 'Stone, according to information furnished me by a kinsman, was very clever and cultured, and had advanced beyond the unitarian doctrines of his family' (J. R. Alger, *Englishmen in the French Revolution*). Described as 'a man of abrupt character and original manners, always ready to be of service to others' (C. Coquerel, *Souvenirs de la Révolution*), he was clearly too much for his uncle, whom he encouraged to speculate and who later became bankrupt. John and his brother set themselves up in the sal ammoniac trade and had a successful manufactory at Old Ford, near Hackney, in

London. In the late 1780s he was an active member of the Gravel Pit congregation at Hackney and a friend of Price and Priestley. He was a member of the chapel committee who invited Priestley to minister there on the death of Price in 1791. Letters between Stone and Priestley on politics and Unitarianism cover the period 1790 to 1802; the publication of some of these in 1798 caused a storm.

However, this important correspondence cannot really be put in context without an understanding of preceding events. Stone was undoubtedly an ardent revolutionary. In October 1790 he presided at a dinner given by the Society of Friends of the Revolution (the Revolution of 1688 in England) for a deputation from Nantes. They wrote home that he was thoroughly acquainted with all the European languages and literature, and that on dining at his house in Hackney they had met the leading men of letters. The poet Samuel Rogers (1763–1855), who had close Unitarian associations, may have been of the number, for he knew Stone well, and twelve months later, dining with him, 'met Fox, Sheridan, Talleyrand, Madame de Genlis and Pamela "radiant with beauty"' (Alger, *op. cit.*, p. 64).

Early in 1792 Stone went to France to establish a sal ammoniac factory there. But his interest in the Revolution was such that this business venture could only have been one element in his decision to leave England. Once in France, he embraced all aspects of the Revolution. On the arrest of British subjects in the autumn of 1793, in retaliation for the capture of Toulon by the British navy, he was imprisoned for 17 days in the Luxembourg. He was again arrested with his wife, Rachel Coope, in April 1794, probably on account of his radical sympathies, but was released on condition of quitting France. He accordingly went to Switzerland, but was speedily allowed to return to Paris, and in June 1794 obtained a divorce from his wife.

Early in 1794 he provided a French agent, an Irish-American clergyman named *William Jackson (1737–1795), with a letter of introduction to his brother in London. Subsequently Jackson was betrayed to the British Government, tried, and – as he was being sentenced to death – poisoned himself in the dock. The trial exposed all the activities of the Stone brothers, and eventually in January 1796 William Stone was tried at the Old Bailey for 'treacherously conspiring with John Hurford Stone, now in France, to destroy the life of the King and to raise a rebellion in his realm'.

Correspondence was read out in court, and the Attorney-General referred to J. H. Stone as that 'seditious and wicked traitor' (W. Cobbett, *State Trials*, Vol. 25, pp. 1155–1438). William had gone the rounds of the literary group so well known to his brother, and had written back to him that if the French invaded they would find none of the sympathy they expected, and such a mission would be doomed to failure. His counsel argued that if promoting an invasion was treason, warding it off must be the reverse.

*William Smith, MP, who later led the Unitarians in many of their Parliamentary activities, gave evidence on William Stone's behalf, for which he was attacked at several later elections at Norwich. Samuel Rogers, who also under examination had to admit that he had known John Stone for many years, in effect spoke up for William, but he was clearly rattled by the experience. The name of Helen Williams came up during the trial, which did not help matters. However, William was acquitted, but by this time he had been financially ruined. He was thus forced to go to France, where after all the excitement he became the overseer of a paper-hanging factory, eventually becoming steward to a country gentleman. John would scarcely have been acquitted, for it was considered that he had led his easily influenced brother into his foolish activities, and in a letter read out at the trial he spoke throughout of the French as 'we' and of the English as 'you', thus identifying himself, as Chief Justice Kenyon remarked, with France.

Under attack

It was these events, among others, that made the radical dissenters so much disliked in England, as the religious affiliations of the participants were made clear by all concerned. The young *John Bowring, growing up in Exeter, wrote in later life that his grandfather and *Rev. Timothy Kenrick liked to talk together in private because 'in those days, it was not always safe to talk, for Exeter was one of the chosen seats of bigotry and intolerance' (Bowring, 1877) where those that were disliked could be burnt in effigy.

One of those that the burghers of Exeter would certainly have burnt in effigy was Joseph Priestley. William Stone passed on to him letters from his brother, and Priestley replied directly to John in Paris. In November 1796, John confirmed a report that Dr. Priestley intended to settle in France. Priestley, he said, would have made France his home in 1794 but for the Terror, and Stone was keeping his books for him. However, it was in 1798 that the most contentious letters between the two were taken off a Danish ship on the high seas by an English ship and brought to London. Addressed to Dr. Priestley in America, they were from both John and Helen and were couched in affectionate terms. Published by 'Peter Porcupine' (*William Cobbett), they created a storm at the time, especially as John, reflecting on the future state of the nation, asks Priestley to fix his residence in England: 'such England as will then be'. Cobbett adds: 'A recommendation with which the Doctor may possibly not yet think it prudent to comply'. Helen concludes a chatty letter with 'My mother and sister are well, and I have two charming little nephews—the eldest is already an excellent republican' (*Copies of Letters Written to Dr Priestley Taken on Board of a Neutral Vessel,* 1798). Such sentiments could hardly have much attraction for the people of Exeter and their like.

Figure 4. A caricature of Joseph Priestley, c. 1785, showing him trampling on the Bible and burning documents representing English freedom.

The caption reads: 'Doctor Phlogiston, the Priestley politician or the Political Priest!' (Artist unknown; Wikimedia Commons)

The furore created by the publication of the letters prompted Dr. Priestley to reply to Cobbett, stating that 'Mr. John Stone was a member of my congregation at Hackney, and a zealous friend of the American and French Revolutions, which sufficiently accounts for his corresponding with me. But I am not answerable for what he, or any other person, may think proper to write to me.' Cobbett then analysed every word of this letter in print and poured scorn on the whole thing. He made comments concerning the Gravel Pit congregation:

> *I not only allow that Stone's being a member of your congregation*
> *sufficiently accounts in the most satisfactory manner, for his becoming*
> *a traitor. This circumstance must convince the few who yet doubt on the*
> *subject that your conventicle at Hackney was a most convenient and*
> *successful school for treason.*
>
> (P. Porcupine, 1799)

On the 1796 trial Cobbett says, lamenting the verdict, 'when all these indubitable, concurrent and striking facts stare us in the face, we are not, like a Westminster Jury, to be cozened out of our conviction by a miserable Unitarian subterfuge'.

But the affair did not stop the correspondence between the two men. To Mr. Russell of Middleton, Priestley wrote: 'I have lately heard from Mr Stone and find that he has not seen my *Comparison*' (4 April 1801). To Stone himself (19 February 1802):

> *At length I have had the satisfaction I had almost despaired of, to receive*
> *a letter from you, and one that interests me exceedingly; especially with*
> *respect to the ecclesiastical state of France and the character of the*
> *Emperor of Russia from whom I now expect great things. I am concerned*
> *that you had not received my letters, especially by Mr. Letombe, the late*
> *Consul ... Your undertaking to translate and publish my History of the*
> *Corruptions of Christianity is very flattering to me, and I hope will do*
> *some good, probably more than my being with you ... If I should come, I*
> *should be happy to be under the same roof with you.*

Again to Stone (1802):

> *I must again say how much satisfaction I received from the various*
> *interesting particulars in your letter. I have sent a copy of part of it to*
> *Mr. Jefferson [the US President], as the information it contains would be*
> *useful and interesting to him, and could not be injurious to you. ...Your*
> *last contains a valuable and pleasing article respecting the spread of*
> *Unitarianism in Germany.*
> (See J. Rutt, Works of Priestley, Vol. 2, pp. 458, 474, 476–7).

Writing in 1799 to the inhabitants of Northumberland, USA, Priestley
further demonstrates his sympathy with John Stone:

> *Mr. Stone is a person who, together with myself, earnestly wished for a*
> *reformation of abuses in the English government, in order to prevent*
> *an entire revolution, which he did not think was wanted there. He now*
> *sees, or thinks he sees, that no such revolution is expected, and therefore*
> *wishes a revolution to take place, thinking it to be absolutely necessary for*
> *the good of the people. I own that I am now inclined to his opinion.*
> (See Rutt, op. cit., Vol 25, p. 31.)

The continuing salon

Despite all the controversy (or maybe because of it), the Williams/Stone
salon held each Sunday evening in Paris attracted not only leading
Frenchmen of the day but also the visiting English in large numbers.
'I have frequently dined with her at Paris, when Kosciusko and other
celebrated persons were of the party,' wrote Samuel Rogers. 'As we were
walking through the Tuilleries, who should we meet, full plump, but my
old friend Stone of Hackney, walking with HM Williams, authoress of the
Letters on France. I was fairly caught, for I have avoided Stone ever since
my arrival, not that I know anything to his prejudice, but that I guard the
incognito. He made me promise to call on him tomorrow ... Dined very
pleasantly with Stone and H M Williams. All our politics English. Stone

was very hearty but HM Williams is Miss Jane Bull completely' (*Wolfe Tone, *Autobiography*, Vol. 2, p. 86).

The diarist *Henry Crabb Robinson (1775–1867), who in later life was an active Unitarian, first visited Helen's much-reduced salon in 1814 but reports in his diary for 4 September 1814: 'In spite of the defamatory reports so maliciously, and perhaps unwarrantably, circulated, Mrs. Barbauld told me that if Miss Williams came to England she should invite her to stay in her house. Mrs. Clarkson and the Wordsworths and numerous ladies visited her all her life' (MS at Dr Williams's Library). 'Miss Williams maintained intimate relations with her English friends, was familiar with the great lights of the Revolution, and her conversation was most instructive, entertaining and varied' (Bowring, 1877). But others found the salons rather different, and found Helen in particular a shade unusual. 'Reichardt, who met Bishop Grégoire and Kosciusko at her house, describes her as wearing a cap with long flaps covering the cheeks, and with a large bouquet falling down from her hair to her nose, so that with her constant nods and gesticulations there were only occasional glimpses of her eyes and mouth' (Alger, 1904, pp. 141, 231).

Even respectable Unitarian ministers visiting Paris found it necessary to meet her. *Rev. **William Shepherd**, Unitarian minister at Gateacre, presented a letter of introduction to her in 1802 and 'was invited to tea on Tuesday evening, which I readily accepted' (Shepherd, 1814, p. 63).

In decline

After 1802 these two brilliant stars were distinctly on the wane. Up to this time finance had been plentiful, for Helen had an income from her books, and John had started afresh in 1795 in business and became one of the chief printers of Paris (he printed the government tax papers). In 1801, he wrote and published under the name of Photinus a letter to du Fossé in defence of Unitarianism. He brought out an edition of the Geneva Bible in 1805 and published several English reprints, but a costly edition of Humboldt's Travels ruined him and by 1813 he was in poor circumstances. An added burden were the two sons of Helen's widowed sister Cecilia, who had died in 1798, whom Helen promised to bring up. She admired the Bonaparte of Brumaire but loathed the later Bonaparte, and was punished by him with a visit and a night's captivity for ignoring him in her *Ode to the Peace* of 1802. She was thus prudently quiet until after the fall of Napoleon in 1815 and welcomed the Restoration, with the English visitors who followed in its train.

To prove that she could do nothing right, she was accused of a *volte face* by some for her changed attitude towards the monarchy. Lady Morgan, in 1816, found numerous guests at her Sunday evening reception, but John Stone was an increasing embarrassment to her, and she had to write no longer for pleasure but to eke out her resources. Crabb Robinson in his diary now presents a very different picture of her: 'Miss Williams is an old maid; Mrs Clarkson thinks she must have been handsome ... I see no traces of her former beauty. Her features are strongly marked: her chin is very long, and an almost perpetual smile does not bring it within ordinary bounds' (20 August 1814). Both Helen and John became French citizens in 1817, but he died in May 1818, apparently a shadow of his former self.

Henry Crabb Robinson had dealings with her again in 1819: 'During the spring of this year Helen Maria Williams applied to me to procure the publication of a volume of *Letters on the State of Politics in France*. She had formerly written *Letters giving an account of the first French Revolution*, a popular work in its day. Alas! the times have changed and she too. After much trouble and application I with difficulty persuaded Robert Baldwin to publish the volume, but she got no money by it, and the house I fear, lost a great deal. I had much to do in correcting the gallicisms of the style. Poor lady! She has been long dead in poverty ... Her connection with Stone, the traitor, whether justly or not, had injured her character' (Morley, 1938, Vol. 1, p. 232).

One of her nephews, Athanase Coquerel, now a pastor in Holland, heard of her poor condition and brought her to Amsterdam. But Dutch life and separation from friends made her melancholy. Her nephew had to take her back to Paris, where he settled a small annuity on her, but she died soon after her return, on 15 December 1827. She was buried in Paris beside John Stone, a largely forgotten figure, although *The Times* did print a short laudatory obituary.

Today Helen is remembered only for her literary connections and her political writings, which 'are worth reading, not as history of events, but of one, and that an important, phase of opinion and thought' (*DNB* entry). Her verses used as hymns were not forgotten, and it was for these that she was known into the twentieth century, mainly in Unitarian collections. 'While Thee I seek, protecting Power' dates from 1786, was first introduced in Dr. Priestley's Birmingham collection of 1790, and was included in most Unitarian collections until *Hymns of Worship Revised* (1962). Altered versions of the hymn were included in some nineteenth-century Congregational collections (see *Julian's Hymnology*, second edition, 1907).

The Coquerel brothers

The continuance of the Protestant tradition in her nephews was in a large measure due to the influence of Helen Williams and J. H. Stone. Bowring (*op. cit.*) commented: 'Her Protestantism was inherited from ancestors who had fought under the flag of the Covenant. But she was no Calvinist and she had a horror of what she often referred to as "the spirit of the priesthood".' She raised two nephews in the freer Protestant tradition. She 'frequently attended the spacious Protestant church of Monsieur Marron in Paris with a mind touched and elevated with devotion' (M. Ray Adams, 1939, pp. 87–117). Undoubtedly John Stone had a great influence on her religious ideas. He was an assertive and advanced Unitarian, and in a letter to du Fossé on Unitarianism he speaks in praise of Priestley and his religious ideas. Here he rejects the divinity of Jesus: 'By whom will the vacancies in the priesthood be filled, when the young men, who in this century of enlightenment are learning to think for themselves right from the first stages of their educational careers, are obliged to assent to dogmas which are so alien to their beliefs and to which they can only subscribe with a sigh or a smile?' (Woodward, *op. cit.*).

For Helen Williams, happiness consisted in political and religious liberty in all things. It was these ideas that were inculcated in her two nephews, Athanase and Charles Coquerel; both became important figures in French Protestantism in later life. Athanase was a leading pastor both in Holland and in France.

John Hurford Stone contributed to their liberal religious inheritance, as the Coquerel brothers generously admitted. Although by any standards an incautious and impulsive man, his aim remained throughout his life the establishment of rational political and religious thought. He wrote to *Theophilus Lindsey on Christmas Day 1801, asking about a certain British religious group who had approached him to support their work in Paris. Being a Unitarian, he felt that they were probably evangelical and would get a shock if he stated his true opinions. The letter was published in the *Monthly Repository* in 1816 by J. T. Rutt, but even at that date Stone's reputation was such that its authorship was left unstated, though no doubt widely known by many readers. After discussing Priestley and Unitarianism in Germany, John defends himself:

> *I say nothing respecting myself except to observe, that whatever my former friends in England (for I do not presume I have any now left) think of my conduct, there are very few points, and these points of prudence, in which I do not feel the most perfect self-approbation—I have laboured, not against England, but for the establishment of rational liberty in France without which it would have been lost in the heart of Europe. Happily for England, for France, and the world, our efforts have not been in vain.*

Sources

Adams, M. R., 1939, in *Wordsworth and Coleridge. Studies in Honour of G. M. Harper*, Princeton USA.

Alger, J. G., 1889, *Englishmen in the French Revolution*.

Alger, J. G., 1904, *Napoleon's British Visitors and Captives 1801–15*.

Anti-Jacobin Review, 1801.

Bowring, J., 1877, *Autobiographical Recollections* (with a brief memoir by L. B. Bowring).

Clayden, P. W., 1887, *Early Life of Samuel Rogers*.

Cobbett, W., 1809, *A Complete Collection of State Trials and Proceedings for High Treason*, Vol. 25.

Copies of Original Letters Recently Written by Persons in Paris to Dr. Priestley in America. Taken on Board of a Neutral Vessel, 1798. (http://archive.org/stream/2573026R.nlm.nih. gov/2573026R#page/n3/mode/2up).

Coquerel, C. *Souvenirs de la Révolution, traduits de l'Anglais de H.M. Williams.*

Dictionary of National Biography.

Dyce, A. (ed.), 1856, *Recollections of the Table Talk of Samuel Rogers.*

Funck-Brentano, F., 1929, introduction to H. M. Williams's *Memoirs of the Reign of Robespierre.*

Gentleman's Magazine, January 1796.

Morley, J. (ed.), 1938, *Henry Crabb Robinson on Books and their Writers.*

Porcupine, Peter, 1799, *Remarks on Explanation published by Dr Priestley on intercepted letters from J. H. Stone.*

Rutt, J. T. (ed.), 1817–31, reprinted in 1972, *The Theological and Miscellaneous Works of Joseph Priestley,* London.

de Selincourt, E. (ed.), 1939, *The Letters of William and Dorothy Wordsworth.*

Shepherd, W., 1814, *Paris in 1802 and 1814.*

Spears, R., 1876, *Record of Unitarian Worthies.*

Todd, F. M., 1948, 'Wordsworth, Helen Maria Williams and France', *The Modern Language Review,* pp. 454–64.

Tone, W. *Autobiography,* Vol. 2.

Woodward, L.D., 1930, *Une Anglaise Amie De La Révolution Francaise: Hélène-Maria Williams et ses Amis,* Paris.

First published in the *Transactions of the Unitarian Historical Society,* 1979.

The
Nineteenth
Century

4 Radical nonconformity in Hackney, 1805–1845

The history of the New Gravel Pit Unitarian Congregation at Hackney is a remarkable one, and its importance can in part be recognised by the eminence of its successive ministers in the period up to 1805: *Richard Price (1770–1791), *Joseph Priestley (1791–1794), and *Thomas Belsham (1794–1805), who were in the vanguard of contemporary theological and political thought.

The New Gravel Pit Hackney congregation played a significant role in the development of Unitarianism in the first half of the nineteenth century. Much has been written of the ministers, but much less about the members of the congregation who in the period up to 1850 were almost as remarkable as their minister, *Rev. Robert Aspland (1782–1845), who served there from 1805 to 1845. This period is important, both in the history of the congregation and in the evolution of Unitarianism. Many of the Chapel members were well known in the social, political, and religious circles of the time; it was a congregation of leading figures in their respective fields.

The year 1806 has been seen as a watershed in the history of radical English political thought. It was the end of a drawn-out period of repression in Britain arising out of the anxiety created by the French Revolution of 1789, and the commencement of an era when the thinking of radicals, both theological and political, became a notable factor nationally. This change came about around the time that Aspland arrived at Hackney. To have chosen such a young unknown man with limited ministerial experience after three ministries of consequence was a brave decision – and, as it transpired, a wise one. A deputation of 24 principal members asked him to come, and after some delay he eventually took up his ministry in June 1805. 'Not everyone was entirely satisfied, since the taste of some of the aged members of the society had been formed on a model of preaching very different from his and it was far from unanimous' (Aspland, p. 177). However, all was soon well and by 1807 any difficulties had, in the main, been overcome.

Figure 5. Robert Aspland (1782–1845)
(Harris Manchester College, Oxford)

Robert Aspland was a mine of industry. He founded and edited the first recognisably Unitarian journals: the *Monthly Repository* from 1806 to 1826, and the *Christian Reformer* (a monthly journal, simpler in presentation and in intellectual content than the *MR*) from 1815 to 1845. Aspland was the main mover of the Unitarian Fund (a denominational supporter of congregations prior to the formation of the British and Foreign Unitarian Association) and served as its first Secretary (1806–1818); he was the founder and principal (1812–1818) of the Unitarian Academy, which trained students for the ministry; founder (1817) and chairman of the Non-Con Club, a dining and discussion association for members of the congregation and their friends; and a trustee and manager (1821–1845) of the Presbyterian Fund, which since the 1690s had supported mainly radical religious congregations and their ministers. In addition he was the main mover in the foundation (1809) of the Christian Tract Society, which distributed Unitarian literature; and he served as the Secretary of the B&FUA, 1835–1841.

Aspland played the major role in the creation of organised Unitarianism in Britain, which he could have achieved only with the backing of a supportive and active congregation. His achievement is all the more notable for the fact that he had a serious heart disease which forced him to take long periods of rest.

The Hackney scene

The congregation which appointed Robert Aspland, fresh from his short ministry at Newport, Isle of Wight, was eager to get him interested in their intellectual pursuits, 'of which he willingly partook with very keen relish' (Aspland, 1850, p. 201). Hackney itself was rich in intellectual nonconformists, who looked on the Gravel Pit as a centre of free religion. Hackney possessed an ideological and symbolic weight far greater than most provincial towns where dissenters held local political power. About three miles north of London itself, it was not only an important centre of dissenting influence, but also one of the wealthiest areas in the country. Writing in 1772, William Maitland *(History of London,* Vol. 2, p. 1366) noted that Hackney 'excels all other Villages in the Kingdom, and probably upon Earth, in the Riches and Opulence of its inhabitants' (quoted in Burley, 2014). The area consisted of suburban retreats for merchants who could afford to live at the distance of a coach drive from the office or warehouse.

Aspland's first residence was near the Chapel in Hackney Terrace, while many of the leaders of the congregation lived a little way away in Hackney Road, Cambridge Heath, and also around Tower Hamlets and Clapton. They were part of the nonconformist set who held many political and social ideas in common. Few advocated revolutionary ideals at home; they were in the main merchants who saw the need for change that would enable them to take a greater role in political affairs. They were united in their belief in religious liberty for all, and they campaigned for penal reform.

Perhaps the chief figure in the congregation from the start of the century until 1840 was *John Towill Rutt (1760–1841). He was chairman of the congregation (later treasurer) in 1805, having been a member since 1796; it was he who was mainly responsible for Aspland coming at all. A radical political activist, he edited the works of his friend Dr. Priestley in 25 volumes. Rutt also wrote many other works, including a compilation entitled *Unitarian Liturgies;* these were used by the congregation when no minister was available.

Rutt was a prolific correspondent to the *Monthly Repository,* and sometimes 'took upon himself the editorial duties' (Aspland, *op.cit.,* p. 192). He participated in the funds and activities that Aspland created for the Unitarian movement, and was one of the main supporters of the London Domestic Mission Society in the 1830s, created by Unitarians to provide a form of social support for the poor. He was educated by *Dr. Joshua Toulmin at Taunton and at St. Paul's School, London, and it was only the noncomformist conscience of his father that prevented Rutt from going to a University. A drug merchant, he had the ability to write clearly on the early years of dissent, as well as having the income to enable him to give the congregation strong financial support.

Another key figure in the congregation was *Samuel Parkes** (1761–1825). A chemist, he wrote manuals on chemistry for the lay person that were translated into several languages. He lived in Durham House, Hackney Road (Aspland moved into this house in 1812 when Parkes moved to a larger house) and had been an active Unitarian since 1793. He regularly took part in the weekly conferences on religious subjects that were held in the chapel from 1807 onwards. These, judging from contemporary accounts, were very similar to modern church discussion groups and attracted people of a wide variety of belief and unbelief.

Leading figures in the congregation spoke at these meetings, and also ministers from nearby Unitarian congregations. So successful were they at recruiting new Unitarians that the Anglican curate at Hackney attacked Aspland for allowing 'unchastised imagination' to reign (Aspland, *op.cit.,* p. 201) Not only did the protagonists for Christianity speak, but also liberal Jews, whom the congregation were willing to welcome into their midst. While he lived in East London, the Jewish economist *David Ricardo (1772–1823) often invited Aspland to dine with him and regularly attended the chapel until he moved to West London.

Another speaker at the religious conferences was *Edgar Taylor (1793–1839). A solicitor by profession, he wrote several standard law books of the day, together with translations from the German of works such as *Grimm's Fairy Tales*. Taylor lived in Hackney Road and married the daughter of **John Christie** (1775–1858), a succesful merchant and a member of the congregation both when Aspland was appointed and when he died. Christie and Taylor were original members of the committee of the Unitarian Fund, and Christie was for many years its treasurer. Edgar's brother, *Richard Taylor (1781–1858), a printer and naturalist, was also connected with the chapel and was Secretary of the Unitarian Academy. A third brother, *John Taylor FRS (1779–1863), was a leading mining engineer and is buried in the chapel yard. All three are recorded in the *Oxford DNB* as sons of *John Taylor (1750–1826), the hymn writer, and great-grandsons of *Rev. John Taylor (1694–1761), during whose ministry the notable Octagon Chapel at Norwich, which became Unitarian, was built.

Rev. John Bickerton Dewhurst (1770–1812) was a speaker at the conferences, a member of the congregation, a committee member, and Classical Tutor of the Unitarian Academy. He was an indifferent minister and in poor health, so he retired into teaching, living with the family of **E. L. Mackmurdo** (died 1817), who were also members of the chapel. Dewhurst was a regular contributor to the *Athenaeum, Annual Review,* and the *Monthly Repository*.

The Flower family

*Benjamin Flower (1755–1829) was associated with Aspland before the latter came to Hackney. He had connections with the congregation but is unlikely to have joined in the theological discussion, for he sat loosely within Unitarianism, consistently maintaining his Baptist associations. His numerous articles in the *Monthly Repository* argued against what he saw as theological excesses. From 1791 he edited the *Cambridge Intelligencer,* which was pro-revolutionary and radical. In 1799 he was imprisoned for libel, and Eliza Gould, one of his readers, was so upset that she visited him in prison; they married on his release. He wrote extensively and was much in the public eye because of his views.

S. K. Ratcliffe in *The Story of South Place,* p. 20, states: 'Benjamin Flower was given to occasional preaching and was known to the leaders of his denomination and naturally to the families living around Hackney, where his daughters were welcome visitors.' His daughters were *Eliza Flower (1803–1846), a composer of music, particularly hymn tunes, and *Sarah Flower Adams (1805–1848), whose hymn *Nearer My God to Thee* is to be found in a wide range of hymn books. Up to 1827, when Flower moved to nearby Dalston, they all lived in Hackney Road. To quote S. K. Ratcliffe again: 'The Hackney–Dalston circle was, at that time [i.e. up to 1830], a characteristic example of cultivated nonconformity, keenly interested in music and literature. The households found a common bond in Shakespeare readings.'

From about 1819 *Rev. W. J. Fox (1786–1864) was living in Hackney, having been the minister of Parliament Court Chapel since 1817. He had many contacts with the congregation and the Non-Con Club and was involved in the running of the *Monthly Repository,* of which he became sole editor in 1831. He married **Eliza Florence** in 1820; they settled in Hackney, but they became estranged, and in 1834 he became associated with the Flower sisters. It was during this period that Benjamin Flower's daughters developed their friendship with *Robert Browning, the poet, which later brought him in contact with Fox and the *Monthly Repository.* S. K. Ratcliffe (*op. cit.,* p. 21) adds:

> Browning's father was a clerk at the Bank of England, and was not an infrequent visitor to the home of a colleague in Hackney. There he found a social atmosphere more liberal than he was accustomed to in South London. Robert often walked over from Camberwell, enjoying the sights of the City en route. He joined the Flower daughters at the piano and read poetry including his own juvenilia. The sisters found him irresistible.

Other leading figures

Also associated with the congregation in the 1820s was *(Sir) Thomas Noon Talfourd (1795–1854), whose father was a member. In later life he became a leading advocate and judge, drama critic, and Member of Parliament. Until 1822, when he married the daughter of J. T. Rutt, he was much engaged in the Hackney nonconformist group.

Other powerful figures in the congregation included **Rev. James Holt** (1756–1828), who joined the congregation in 1818, after many years as a minister. In his will he left money to set up a charity to assist students for the Unitarian ministry; it still exists today. Another attender, although probably not a member, was *Dr. Thomas Cogan (1736–1818) , who had been a minister in the English Church at Rotterdam and in Southampton. He was awarded a doctorate in medicine by the University of Leyden in 1767 (there were a number of medical men in the Hackney congregation) and after that he went back and forth to Holland until he settled in Clapton and London in 1810. His main claim to fame was that he founded, with Dr. W. Hawes, the Royal Humane Society in 1774. His relative, *Rev. Eliezer Cogan (1762–1855), who had connections with the Hackney congregation and was eventually buried in the graveyard there, kept a successful boarding school at Walthamstow from 1801 to 1828, at which *Benjamin Disraeli, a future Prime Minister, and the surgeons Gilbert Mackmurdo and *Samuel Solly FRS were educated.

The barrister **Christopher Richmond** (1786–1832) was a member of the Chapel Committee and treasurer of the associated Non-Con Club. Richmond gave legal advice to the nonconformists who successfully agitated for the repeal in 1828 of the Test and Corporation Acts, which penalised dissenters in a variety of ways, and for Catholic emancipation in 1829. He was a 'valued and accomplished friend' of Aspland (Aspland, *op. cit.,* p. 517). **Rev. James Pickbourn** (1735–1814) kept a school at Hackney, was a member of the congregation and Librarian of Dr Williams's Library, the London dissenting institution. In another sphere completely, an active member was **John Martineau** (1758–1834), head of Whitbread's Brewery in the City, who lived at nearby Stamford Hill. **William Lawrence**, whose family had a notable impact on Unitarianism later in the century, became a member in the 1830s (see the article on the Lawrence family in this volume).

Among other attenders at the chapel were **Rev. William Friend** (1757–1841), the Cambridge divine-turned-Unitarian who became an actuary after ejection from the University, and *John (later Sir) **Bowring** (1792–1872), the linguist, writer, traveller, and MP. Bowring lived in Hackney and attended the chapel with his family, some of whom are buried in the chapel yard. Bowring wrote more than 60 poems for the *Monthly Repository* and did translations, for he had command of several languages. In 1816 he married **Maria Lewin**, the daughter of **Samuel Lewin** (died 1823), a member of the Chapel. It is probable that Bowring was a member of the congregation for a period.

Non-Unitarians

Others who participated in the Hackney nonconformist group were not connected with the chapel or with Unitarianism. *Rev. Samuel Palmer (1741–1813) ministered to a large dissenting congregation meeting in Mare Street, Hackney, and was its minister for fifty years. Differences in theology did not narrow his sympathies, for he was a friend of Aspland and a contributor to his journals. Robert Aspland's son, *Rev. R. Brook Aspland**, recalled that as a child he met 'three divines of most venerable and attractive appearance in the clerical costume of the last century, one of whom was Mr. Palmer who in a manner combining dignity, kindness and pleasantry, gave him his blessing, and wished him to be like his father in everything, except his heresy' (Aspland, *op. cit.*, p. 233). Palmer was even friendly enough to quieten noisy children at the laying of the foundation stone of the new Unitarian meeting house in 1810.

Another trinitarian nonconformist was *Rev. Dr. J. Pye Smith (1774–1851), the theological tutor (1806–1851) at Homerton College, a ministerial training college. He was a Congregational minister who responded to Unitarian arguments in religious journals. He and his pupils attended the inauguration of the new New Gravel Pit Chapel in 1810, and when the chapel was having a new roof put on in 1824, he kindly offered the loan of the Old Gravel Pit Chapel during refurbishments. (The meeting house that served the congregation from 1810 until 1857 was a poor structure and the repairs of 1824 cost £1,500.) Although relations with Dr. Smith were good, they were not that good, and the offer was gratefully declined.

The Non-Con Club

A congregation which could attract so many people of culture, learning, and position had considerable financial resources at their command. The new meeting house, erected in 1810, cost £4,200, which was £1,500 in excess of the estimate, but this large sum was found quite quickly, even in a period of national economic difficulty. The membership of the Non-Con Club, founded in July 1817 at Aspland's home, consisted mainly of subscribers to the Chapel. Members read papers on subjects connected with nonconformity. During Parliamentary sittings, liberal members of the House of Commons and distinguished foreigners (including the Indian religious reformer Rammohun Roy) were occasionally invited as guests. *Dr. Southwood Smith, *Benjamin Wood, MP, *Rev. John Kenrick, and *George Dyer, the author, were among Club members (see *TUHS*, 1969 for a fuller account of the Non-Con Club).

Such a collection of notable people could not be found in similar dissenting congregations after 1850. The climate of the age was different: the dissenters' grievances had been redressed, and legal regulations penalising Jews were soon to be abolished in 1858. The resplendent learned figures of the 1820s were not to be replaced. Hackney was becoming one of the inner suburbs of London; the City could be reached quickly by train, so the richer families tended to move further out. But Aspland had laid solid foundations, and the congregation continued to be large and to attract the wealthy. A new larger church was erected in 1858, in the Gothic-revival style. However, even as the congregation increased up until the 1870s, the vitality, striving, and learning among its members in the early nineteenth century could not be matched in its subsequent history.

Sources

Aspland, R. B., 1850, *Life of Robert Aspland* (his father).

Burley, S., 2014, *Hazlitt the Dissenter, Religion, Philosophy and Politics 1766–1816*, Palgrave Macmillan.

Christian Reformer 1832.

Green, E. H., 1913, *A Short History of the New Gravel Pit Sunday School*.

McLachlan, H., 1931, *English Education under the Test Acts*.

McLachlan, H., 1934, *The Unitarian Movement in the Religious Life of England*.

Monthly Repository, 1812.

Meynell, W., 1904, *Benjamin Disraeli*.

Mineka, F., 1944, *The Dissidence of Dissent*, University of Carolina Press USA.

New Gravel Pit Chapel Burial Register, at Dr Williams's Library, London.

Ratcliffe, S. K., 1955, *The Story of South Place*.

Rutt, J. T., 1801, *Liturgies for Unitarian Worship*.

TUHS 1924, 1928.

Unitarian Almanacs, *passim*.

Whitehead, J. T., 1889, *Historical Sketch of the Chapel*.

Note

The congregation of the New Gravel Pit Unitarian Chapel Hackney terminated in 1969 as a result of an Act of Parliament granting compulsory-purchase powers to the then Greater London Council. The building was demolished in the early 1970s. The Council built blocks of flats on part of the site, but the graveyard and its memorials remain as a closed green site (2014). The proceeds of the sale were brought together in the New Gravel Pit Hackney Chapel Trust Fund to benefit Unitarian congregations in the London Borough of Hackney and the London and South-East area. The nearby building occupied by the congregation up to 1810 remains, much adapted, in commercial use (2015).

First published in *Transactions of the Unitarian Historical Society*, 1967.

5 The Chamberlains and Unitarianism

I (still) think it unseemly that a Unitarian should have the predominant voice in the appointment of Bishops.

Thus wrote *Lord Hugh Cecil, a leading Anglican and the then Provost of Eton College, expressing himself strongly in *The Times* on 15 February 1938 about the appointment of bishops of the Church of England by the Prime Minister, *Neville Chamberlain. The controversy had arisen over a new measure presented to the Church Assembly, requiring Deans and Chapters to elect the person nominated by the Prime Minister as bishop. In the debate on the measure, designed to replace a Tudor enactment, Cecil stated: 'If we lived in the reign of Henry VIII a Unitarian would not be in Downing Street. He would be burned at Smithfield' (*Times*, 9 February 1938). Cecil did not deny Chamberlain's conscientiousness in performing the task, but he thought it 'scandalous and intolerable' that a Unitarian should appoint bishops of the Church of England.

Hugh Cecil, later Baron Quickswood, was stringent in asserting his view of Unitarians, who refused to adhere to creeds and generally held heterodox theological views which from his standpoint were inconsistent with the faith of the Anglican Church. He did not see how they could have any form of relationship with the Church of England, although the liberal Anglicans took a different view about some leading Unitarians. In 1933 Cecil had been mainly responsible for arraigning the Dean of Liverpool before the York Assembly of the Church of England for allowing Unitarians (*L. P. Jacks and Lawrence Redfern) to preach in the Cathedral. This created considerable public controversy, both in religious circles and in the newspapers, some of it fostered by the Bishop of Durham, *Herbert Hensley Henson (see *TUHS*, 2000 and Henson's autobiography (Henson 1942 and 1950)).

Was Cecil right in asserting that Neville Chamberlain was a Unitarian? Most Prime Ministers claim a Christian affiliation, although the religious credentials of some have been slight, to say the least. Most biographers state that Neville was a lapsed Unitarian – but in what sense was Neville Chamberlain a Unitarian at all? To what extent was his elder brother *Austen a practising adherent of Unitarianism? To what extent was the brothers' attitude to religion affected by their dominant and obviously Unitarian father Joseph, who had lost his personal faith after the death of his second wife in 1875?

The Unitarian background

*Joseph Chamberlain was a Unitarian born and bred, a fact of which he was openly proud. Whatever his personal beliefs may have been after the deaths of his first two wives, Joseph remained a Unitarian in allegiance and public affirmation until his own death in 1914. He was attuned to those aspects of the Unitarian faith that were commonly emphasised in the second half of the nineteenth century: the values of individualism, self-reliance, moral earnestness, and social action. Unitarians were expected to arrive at personal conclusions on the Bible, religious authority, and traditional Christian beliefs, and to act accordingly. Critics in the nineteenth century judged Unitarians and their worship as dry, lacking in emotion, and over-intellectual.

In towns throughout the country Unitarian families were, like the Chamberlains, often leaders in the community, not only in business but also in the fields of educational and social reform. Many were among the richer members of society, and C. M. Trevelyan in his *English Social History* has rightly pointed out that Unitarianism was the religion of the mill owner and not his worker. With the Quakers, Unitarians were considered the aristocracy of English religious dissent.

Their distinctive theology and often strong financial position did not make Unitarians generally popular, so they felt that they were consistently spoken against, mainly by Anglicans, often for social as well as religious reasons. Unitarians therefore concentrated their social and family life on their chapels and meeting houses, many of which dated back to the late seventeenth and early eighteenth centuries. These meeting houses had been mainly English Presbyterian in origin, but their theology had evolved over time, even if the families who supported them for generations remained the same. They tended to intermarry; this applied to dissenters in general, but to Unitarians in particular. The Chamberlains and related families had done this for generations. They were typical among Unitarian families who in the nineteenth century often got richer and became more socially influential with the years, and they were related to, or knew, most of the Unitarian movement's leading figures, and many outside it, in civic affairs. Both of Joseph's parents were avid supporters of their chapels, as in turn their parents had been before them. Joseph Chamberlain senior and his wife **Caroline Harben** came from a long line of radical Protestant dissenters. *J. L. Garvin in his *Life* of Joseph (Vol. I, p. 39) quotes a Chamberlain relation on Joseph senior:

> *The children loved him always except on Sunday mornings when he*
> *put them through a little catechism after service. His religion to him*
> *was the life within the life. When anyone was first introduced he would*
> *sometimes say at once, 'Yes sir, Joseph Chamberlain and a Unitarian.' If*
> *they swallowed that, it was all right.*

If any of his sons would prepare for the Unitarian ministry, Joseph senior promised he would settle upon them £200 a year. He hoped that Joseph junior would take this course, but his son was not tempted, and nor were his brothers.

Family life was centred on Little Carter Lane Chapel in the City of London, a congregation founded in the seventeenth century which migrated to Upper Street Islington in 1862. The Chamberlains were closely associated with the congregation for about 130 years. Garvin points out that not even the House of Commons in later years was more familiar to Joseph than was the interior of this chapel in his youth. Joseph met many prominent Unitarians, and he was of course related to some of them, including ***James Martineau**, the leading Unitarian minister and theologian of the day. In his teens Joseph taught young children from the slums in the chapel's Sunday School mission classes. He was educated at University College School in London from 1850, before entering the long-established family shoe-making business at 36 Milk Street in 1852. This advanced educational establishment attracted the children of leading radical dissenters, some of whom were Joseph's relations.

Garvin is clear on the significant influence that the Little Carter Lane congregation exerted on Joseph: 'Chamberlain's inward life until he was nearly forty was directed by his religious upbringing ...We may find here the germ of his assertive independence; of his anti-official or anti-orthodox initiative throughout his political career; or of his executive force as a leader of social reform' (p. 41). While Garvin overstated the case in claiming that 'Liberal politics followed inevitably from the Unitarian creed', this generalisation very much applied to the Chamberlain and related families.

Figure 6. Joseph Chamberlain (poster published by the Tariff Reform League)
(Wikimedia Commons)

Birmingham

When Joseph was sent to Birmingham to help run the screw-making part of the associated Nettlefold family business in 1854, he joined and was at once active in the New Meeting Birmingham. In 1861, with the erection of a neo-gothic chapel building in Broad Street, its name was changed to the Church of the Messiah, a move which Joseph strongly supported. The congregation was something over one hundred strong, consisting mainly of business men and their families who found meaning in their meeting together in an atmosphere of social and civic commitment. Joseph again became part of a close network of Unitarian families: the Nettlefolds, the Beales, the Rylands, the Martineaus, the Kenricks, and later the Crosskeys, who wielded considerable power and influence within Birmingham. These Unitarian families often intermarried, and cousins formed an extended clan, a tendency which continued into present times. Marriage between often close relations meant complex inter-connections, so much so that a current member of the extended family describes it as not so much a genealogical table, more a piece of knitting.

Deeply involved in New Meeting's finances, Joseph was for a period its treasurer; in addition, he regularly taught evening classes for working men. From 1866 he subsidised the provision of meals under the auspices of the congregation for working children less than 15 years of age, an arrangement which continued for many years. This is shown in the extensive archives of the Church of the Messiah held in Birmingham Reference Library, which consist of some 238 volumes, a source that has tended to be neglected by researchers.

Joseph's loss of faith on the death of his second wife in 1875 is documented by most of his biographers. The emphasis in this article is not on his personal beliefs – he termed himself in his later years 'a reverent agnostic' – but on his continuing membership of the Church of the Messiah, his public identification of himself as a Unitarian after the mid-1870s, and the effect that this may have had on his sons Austen and Neville.

He definitely stopped going to chapel on a regular basis after 1875; but this would have happened anyway, whatever his personal beliefs might have been, as his involvement in city and national politics widened. However, he kept an eye on the ministers at the Church of the Messiah, no doubt through his numerous relations, and on much else that happened at the Birmingham church. Joseph remained one of its principal financial supporters until his death in 1914. A chapel trustee from 1868 until 1913, he retired because of his advanced age and incapacity when a new trust deed was created. Those appointed as ministers of the church had to be inspected by Joseph, who seemed to be always there in the background. **L. P. Jacks**, a well-known preacher, writer, and broadcaster in the next century in both Britain and America, was asked to become its minister in 1894. Jacks was a supporter of Home Rule for Ireland and feared that he would clash with Joseph and his very different views on this major issue. In his autobiography, *Confessions of an Octogenarian* (p.148), Jacks remembers the conversation:

> *'I don't think that matters,' said Thomas Russell, a member of the deputation, 'we are not all of the same mind with Mr Chamberlain.'*
> *'Besides,' added Herbert New, the church treasurer, 'though Mr Chamberlain subscribes liberally to church funds, he very rarely attends.'*
> *'There is a virtue named discretion,' said Mr Beale.' 'I am not sure of possessing it', said I.*

Jacks nevertheless became the Minister and clearly was approved of, as he received regular invitations to the Chamberlains' Birmingham home, 'Highbury', and the contact was later taken over by Austen and Neville. Jacks recalls (p. 156) what could have been a late theological thought from Joseph:

> *Pausing before an orchid of great beauty he pointed out the astonishing arrangement Nature had made for the fertilisation of its flowers. 'And the scientific people tell me that it has come about by chance – Rubbish!'*

Jacks left Birmingham in 1903, but he was not forgotten, for Joseph asked that he should conduct his funeral. This he did at the Church of the Messiah, which, as *The Times* stated, was 'the Unitarian Church where Mr Chamberlain in his younger days taught in the Sunday school, and with which he has been connected ever since' (6 July 1914). There was no address, but the order used was that of King's Chapel Boston in the USA, the oldest Unitarian chapel in America. Joseph's last wife's family, the Endicotts, had religious connections there, though she was an Episcopalian. Joseph never married entirely outside the Unitarian connection, even if this marriage in Washington USA did not take place in a Unitarian church but in a fashionable Episcopal Church. It was attended by the President of the USA and members of the Cabinet and Supreme Court, with the President speaking at the reception (Marsh, p. 312). Chamberlain was an international figure: the Secretary of State for the Colonies in the Conservative Government at the time, and previously a member of the Liberal cabinets of W. E. Gladstone.

Publicly Joseph always maintained that he was a dissenter, although he strongly refused to be called a nonconformist, which he saw as a wider term embracing recently formed religious organisations. For example, he attended a dinner on 19 June 1878 to mark the fiftieth anniversary of the repeal of the Test and Corporation Acts (these enactments had since the seventeenth century prevented dissenters holding many public offices). He gave an address at the centenary of the Church of the Messiah Sunday School in 1888, in which he made it clear that he still regarded himself as a Unitarian:

> *The Unitarian body has never been a proselytising or an aggressive sect,*
> *and I believe its mission is not meant so much to make converts to its own*
> *particular tenets, but rather to liberalise the creed and practice of other*
> *religious bodies ... But that being the principle of our sect it is not likely*
> *that we shall in future devote ourselves to making Unitarians. We have not*
> *established these Sunday schools ... in order to create church members.*
> (*CL*, 13 October 1888)

The Bishop of Birmingham, preaching at the Pro Cathedral on Joseph's death in 1914, stated that 'he was faithful to his own denomination, and was full of sympathy for all honest religious thought' (*CL*, 11 July 1914). *Rev. R. J. Campbell at the City Temple in London said that Chamberlain was 'unswervingly faithful to his religious convictions, and never throughout his brilliant career was tempted to depart from them' (*CL, op. cit.*). An obituary made the point that Joseph had 'fidelity to the stern dictates of the Unitarian faith ... He took his religion seriously – sternly if you like – as a real thing, the core of life, a disciplinary force, entitled to mould action in every department' (*CL, op. cit.*). In many ways Joseph was the quintessential Unitarian of his time and a representative figure within the denomination.

The sons: Austen (1863–1937) and Neville (1869–1940)

The same cannot be said of his two famous sons: the elder, Austen (Chancellor of the Exchequer, Foreign Secretary, and recipient of the Nobel Peace Prize), and Neville (Minister of Housing, Chancellor of the Exchequer, and Prime Minister). They are a unique example in the Western democratic world of a father and two sons holding a succession of such high offices in government.

Neither followed Joseph in support of the Church of the Messiah, although other members of the family remained closely involved until the mid-twentieth century. Joseph's personal religious convictions, though not his affirmation, changed in 1875, when Austen was 12 years old and Neville six, and this dichotomy in their father's attitude no doubt influenced them. They became detached from active participation in the Church of the Messiah at an early age and did not take up membership of other churches or chapels. Neither subscribed to the Church of the Messiah in adult life, though both gave small sums for Sunday School and other benevolent work until the 1930s.

Austen (whose first name was Joseph) remained a nominal Unitarian, above all in recognition of the Chamberlain family tradition, of which he was proud. Austen had lived for decades in the same house as his magisterial parent, whose influence on him was all-embracing. In 1915 he put together, and had privately printed, *Notes on the Families of Chamberlain and Harben* as a labour of devotion, probably as a memorial for his recently deceased father. Affirming the family tradition led him to contribute to the appeal for the refurbishment of the Unity Chapel Islington in 1912 and to be a member of the Unitarian Historical Society. His only known reference to a religious allegiance in later life is contained in a letter of 1928 on the Prayer Book controversy:

> *Scratch me and you find the Nonconformist. I may not be a very orthodox Unitarian if there is such a thing as orthodoxy in that very heterodox body, but in every fibre of my being I am Protestant with the biggest 'P' that you can put to it.*
>
> (Petrie, p. 320)

Austen did not appear to think in religious terms; his faith was bound up in a mixture of family pietas, inescapably nonconformist and Unitarian, and patriotism. Towards the end of his life he wrote in a letter, 'Do you know Cecil Spring Rice's hymn? [*I vow to thee my country*]. It is the perfect expression of the faith in which I have lived' (letter to Ellen Lady Askwith, 15 July 1936, quoted in Dutton, p. 337). It was sung at his funeral.

His cousin **W. Byng Kenrick** perhaps best sums up Austen's position in a short appreciation which appeared in the *TUHS*, 1937, p. 191, the only obituary of substance to appear in a Unitarian publication: 'Sir Austen Chamberlain could not have been described as a practising Unitarian; although, if it had been necessary for him to accept some denominational designation, he would not have taken any other than that into which he had been born.'

Austen's funeral took place at St Margaret's Westminster on 19 March 1937. The Archbishop of Canterbury gave the blessing, and the service was followed by cremation. The memorial service took place at Birmingham Pro Cathedral, and the Provost preached. There was seemingly no mention of the Unitarian connection: he had moved out of the Unitarian sphere, or at least his immediate family had.

The Prime Minister's beliefs

Neville (whose first name was Arthur) was more removed than Austen from even nominal Unitarian allegiance. Apart from funerals, there is no evidence that he attended Unitarian services during his adult life. No obituaries appear in the denominational press. He never claimed to be Christian or religious, nor was he seen as such, and apparently he did not like attending services of worship of any kind. The only religious stand that he seemed to have taken was a refusal as a schoolboy at Rugby public school to face the altar when the Creed was recited; and he later expressed distaste for aspects of the Roman Catholic mass. Incongruously, Neville kept two statues on his desk at home, depicting the Virgin Mary and St John standing at the foot of the cross, which are now in the possession of his grandson, James Lloyd. Mr Lloyd's godmother, a close family friend, recalling these figures (in a letter to the author, July 2003), believes that they may have appealed to him more for artistic than religious reasons, because she always understood him to be agnostic.

The Archbishop of Canterbury, Cosmo Gordon Lang, grew to like Neville as a result of his contact with him as Prime Minister, but he was saddened by his perception of him as a Unitarian with no stated faith. He was not encouraged when Neville used the term 'reverent agnostic' about himself, the phrase coined first by his father. Some writers state that he was a lapsed Unitarian, but there is little evidence to show that he was ever an adherent, even when young. Joseph never required religious adherence of his children, arguing that if family life had not influenced them, someone else could, which was incidentally not an unusual stand for late-nineteenth-century Unitarians to take. Neville's funeral took place in Westminster Abbey (*Oxford DNB*).

Neville retained the background associated with the religious principles taught by his father, which took him in a social and political direction rather than a religious one. Joseph, Austen, and Neville all followed this increasingly secular course, while retaining nineteenth-century Unitarian moral and social attitudes. The tenor of Unitarianism in the mid-nineteenth century centred on a serious concern for the condition of humanity which arose from their belief in a good and kind God, and a conviction that man is not in essence evil, bound for eternal damnation, but is capable of progress. This affirmation had social implications for the commercially successful Unitarians, for, as a cousin of Neville pointed out, 'We always understood as children that as our lives had fallen in pleasant places it behoved us the more to do what we could to improve the lot of those less happily placed' (Dilks, p. 8). Some have claimed that Neville's policy of appeasement towards German aggression when Prime Minister in the 1930s grew, at least in part, out of his horror at the thought that the poorer areas of London would be bombed. In dealing with Hitler, an under-developed sense of evil, a Unitarian attribute, may not have helped.

Joseph developed his own version of the civic gospel, which he passed on to his sons. Nineteenth-century Unitarians emphasised personal reliance in nearly everything, and this attitude was summed up in Joseph's advice to his children: 'Tell the truth, do what you are told but question afterwards if necessary, and if you do something do it well' (Dilks, pp. 19, 32). Rejection of creeds and a cold rationality encouraged a strong personal independence and an anti-authoritarian approach to practical issues. You must bear your own problems – a belief that Joseph and Neville could take to extreme lengths. Unitarians were not encouraged to show emotion or affection in public; this seems to have been a mark of the Chamberlains, although in private family life they could be different.

Neville did make what can be considered a religious comment in his last months as Prime Minister. On 16 April 1940 he paid a visit with his wife to the annual assembly of the National Council of the Evangelical Free Churches held at the City Temple, in the company of the Lord Chancellor Lord Caldecote, an evangelical Christian. He probably only attended such an event on the prompting of the latter. After a few introductory remarks he avoided speaking on an avowedly religious topic, as no doubt was expected. He stated: 'I am afraid today I must not stop to deliver the address which I hoped to. In a few moments I must go back to resume my labours ... Though I must soon leave you, I propose to leave behind me a hostage in the person of my wife ... as a pledge that in happier days you should ask me to come and speak to you again' (*The Times*, 17 April 1940).

However, he then added his views on the war and how it was developing. His comments in many ways encapsulate the nineteenth-century liberal religious ethos in which he was brought up, based on progress, enlightenment, and a belief in the good in humanity. He did not directly adhere to his Unitarian family religion in his mature years, but his closing words in a speech towards the end of his life show that its principles and background moulded and influenced him until the end:

Every day that passes gives us some new demonstration of Germany's
utter disregard of religion, of mercy, of truth and of justice. If they were to
triumph in what they are doing, why then every fortress which has been
built by civilisation upon the principles of Christianity would go down
and the world would relapse into that barbarism which, until a little
while ago, we thought we had buried under centuries of progress ... This
war will be won by the spiritual forces of the world as much as by the
material power of their brave defenders. These spiritual forces have been
affronted by what Germany has done and is doing, and to you, whose
mission it is to uphold and exalt the spiritual life of this country, I appeal,
with confidence to give us your aid to crush the powers of tyranny and
wickedness for ever.

Sources

The Christian Life, October 1888, July 1914.

Church of the Messiah Annual Reports 1911–1914.

Dilks, D., 1984, *Neville Chamberlain*, Vol.1, Cambridge.

Dutton, D., 1985, *Gentleman in Politics*, Bolton.

Garvin, J. L., 1932, *Life of Joseph Chamberlain*.

Henson, H., 1942, *Retrospect of an Unimportant Life*, 1863–1939, Oxford.

The Inquirer, June 1878, February 1902, July 1914.

Jacks, L. P., 1942, *The Confessions of an Octogenarian*.

Kenrick, W. B., 1937, *TUHS*.

Lockhart, J., 1949, *Cosmo Gordon Lang*.

Marsh, P., 1994, *Joseph Chamberlain Entrepreneur in Politics*.

Oxford Dictionary of National Biography.

Petrie, C., 1940, *Life & Letters of Austen Chamberlain*, Vol. 2.

Ruston, A., 1993, *TUHS*.

Tarrant, W.G., 1925, in *Freedom and Truth, Modern Views of Unitarian Christianity*.

The Times, July 1914, March 1937, February 1938, April 1940.

Titford, C., 1912, *History of Unity Church Islington*.

Turner, G., 2000, *TUHS*.

Williamson, P., 2000, *English Historical Review*, June.

Wilson, H. G., 1945, *TUHS*.

From *Transactions of the Unitarian Historical Society 2008*, based on an address given at the Annual Meeting of the Association of Denominational History Societies, November 2006

6 William Ewart Gladstone – a Unitarian connection?

Nobody has ever claimed that William Gladstone (four times Prime Minister in the nineteenth century) was Unitarian in any sense. From his school days, he maintained an orthodox Christian belief based on dogma (he repeatedly claimed that he liked dogma) from which he did not deviate. The force of his religious belief, which helped to create and inform his powerful political and moral affirmations, in turn made him into a nineteenth-century religious symbol. Gladstone was almost worshipped by certain nonconformists, although theologically he could be very different from many of them; a Unitarian example of a committed disciple was the prominent minister *Rev John Page Hopps. A devoted member of the Church of England, Gladstone consistently related his views to Christian faith and dogma and the claims of the established Church, even defending some of its acknowledged anomalies.

Gladstone's religious writings, as with so much else associated with him, were prodigious in quantity. His rejection of the Unitarian position can be found in several places; a representative example, written when he was nearly eighty in May 1888, is contained in his review (in the journal *Nineteenth Century*) of the novel *Robert Elsmere* by Mrs Humphrey Ward:

> A Christianity without Christ is no Christianity; and a Christ
> not divine is one other than the Christ on whom the souls of
> Christians have habitually fed... How then is the work of peace to
> be promoted by the excision from our creed of that central truth on
> which we are generally agreed? The onward movement of negation
> in the present day has presented perhaps no more instructive
> feature than this, that the Unitarian persuasion has, in this country
> at least, by no means thriven on it ... we are informed that the
> numbers of professed Unitarians have increased less than other
> communities.

Gladstone learned his evangelical form of Christianity from his mother, but his dominant father, the highly successful man of business, *Sir John Gladstone (1764–1851), sat more easily in the Christian religious spectrum. David Bebbington has pointed out that as a Scot newly arrived in Liverpool (in 1787) John had naturally attended the Presbyterian Chapel, which by this date was well advanced on the path towards Unitarianism. *Alexander Gordon, perhaps the premier historian of religious dissent of his time, disputed the claim that John was ever a dissenter, finding no record of his religious connection until 1792, when he married and became a trustee of the Oldham Street Kirk (of Scotland) in 1793, and later built two Anglican churches in 1814 in Seaforth. What is clear is that John was not a dedicated Anglican in William Gladstone's terms, or specifically attached to evangelical belief. 'In religion', Sir John wrote in later years, 'but not in politics I am no party man.' According to Bebbington, William was distressed when in his last hours in 1851 his father declined to receive Holy Communion but called for a plate of porridge.

Sitting easily in the denominational divide probably prompted John to send David, his youngest brother, whom he brought him to live with him in 1800, to Manchester College, which was known as a Unitarian foundation. David is said to have attended Renshaw Street Chapel Liverpool and to have become Unitarian.

This article presents examples of William Gladstone's writing and statements in which he considers the Unitarian position. They show that although he was critical of it without question, gradually in later life he adopted a softer view of specific Unitarians and the stands that they took, the chief example being James Martineau.

A wrong marriage

William's first real clash over Unitarianism came in 1835 and put him at variance with most of his family. By that date, following his time at Oxford, he had adopted his strong and assertive faith, despite having friends from more radical religious traditions. As he wrote in later life, 'I was brought up to believe that every Unitarian (I suppose also every heathen) must as a matter of course be lost for ever' (*The PM's Papers*, p. 149). William was therefore aghast at the prospect of his brother Robertson (1805–1875) marrying **Ellen Jones**, the daughter of **Hugh Jones**, a Unitarian banker from Liverpool. This is how in 1897 (*ibid.*) he recalled the incident:

> *As late as the year 1836 one of my brothers married a beautiful and in every way charming person who had been brought up in a family of the Unitarian profession yet under a mother very sincerely religious. I went through much mental difficulty and distress at the time as there had been no express renunciation of the ancestral creed, and absurdly busied myself with devising this or that religious test as what if accepted might suffice.*

> *So, as will be seen, the first access of churchlike ideas to my mind by no means sufficed to expel my inherited and bigoted misconception, though in the event they did it as I hope effectively. But I long retained in my recollection an observation made to me in 1829 by Mrs Benjamin Gaskell of Thornes near Wakefield, a seed which was destined long to remain in my mind without germinating. I fell into religious conversation with this excellent woman, the mother of my Eton friend Milnes Gaskell, and herself the wife of an Unitarian. She said to me, 'Surely we cannot entertain a doubt as to the future condition of any person truly united to Christ by faith and love, whatever may be the faults of his opinions.' Here she supplied me with the key to the whole question. To this hour I feel grateful to her accordingly, for the scope of her remark is very wide: and it is now my rule to remember her in prayer before the altar.*

He made a great fuss about the forthcoming marriage in 1835, which some commentators have argued was prompted more by his own desire to marry (as he did in 1839) than by theological niceties. At the height of the dispute William confides to his diary, 'more and more I felt what a wretched gift I would be as a husband' (*Diary* 23 November 1835). The debate ran on for months. As Gladstone admits, he did not behave well, although his sister Helen gave support. He insisted on a statement of belief from his brother's intended bride (*Diary*, p. 205).

Gladstone prepared a long and detailed statement, not addressed or signed, consisting of over 5,000 words, written late in 1835, now in the Flintshire Record Office (MSS GG1382). Here he states his strong theological objections to his brother's marriage to a Unitarian, seeing their view of sin and human nature as totally at odds with what he called 'our' faith. This was because Unitarians did not believe in the fallen nature of mankind. They may believe that humanity is frail and in need of strength to meet the divine requirements, but Unitarians do not believe that humankind is by nature divorced from God. In support of this he quotes Colossians Chapter 1 verses 21–22, which he saw as the basis of all Christian truth:

> And you, that were sometime alienated and enemies in your mind
> by wicked works, yet now hath he reconciled, in the body of his
> flesh through death, to present you holy and unblameable and
> unreproveable in his sight.

Where this belief was missing, Gladstone could see no real basis on which to assume that Christian truth would triumph.

He had to admit that Ellen Jones was frank and of high conduct, and he did not doubt that her statement of belief which he had required was sincere and should be accepted; he recognised that she was trying to meet his objections. His father and others accepted Ellen's statement, but nevertheless William remained unsatisfied. They had been encouraged by what she had written, but he was clear that his hopes had been dashed. What she had stated was negative in tone, and he argued that it was necessary to critically examine the faith of those who came from a background different from 'ours' and whose friends and relations were alien.

In his diary on 18 November 1835 he notes: 'The letter received from Robertson today unfolds the beliefs of MEJ in her own words. These will satisfy my father and my brothers; nevertheless to me they do not seem to express the first truths of the Gospel, that is, the most necessary truths of all. My sister's feelings accord with my own ... the two of us are sundered from all the rest.'

His father wanted him to give up his objections: 'Once more, for God's sake, reflect on what you may be sowing the seeds of' (letter, 7 December 1844). He responded to his father that he would attend the wedding if his presence was required, but it should not be assumed that if he did this it was in accordance with his personal belief. In another letter Gladstone admits that Robertson thought he should have kept all this to himself, but he had written to his brother Tom that he could do no other. Robertson eventually told William to desist, and he had to withdraw. William was told by his father to attend the wedding, which he did, noting glumly in his diary (Vol. 2, p. 219):

> *27 January 1836: We saw the marriage take place soon after 9. At 10.15 they left L.pool. Would to God that I had been able to lift up my hands to bless them, and to pray for them with an affectionate heart but my [blessing] such as it was, at least got out of my mouth.*

The events of 1844

Gladstone's most well-known point of contact with Unitarianism in political terms came in 1844. His support for their position in Parliament, while he was a Cabinet minister, played a significant role in the passing of the Dissenters' Chapels Act. This Act resolved the longstanding legal dispute over the trusteeship of English Presbyterian chapels and associated funds formed before what is known as the Trinity Act in 1813, which legalised the holding of Unitarian beliefs. Most English Presbyterian Chapels had become Unitarian by the early nineteenth century in terms of the beliefs held by their trustees and members, and opponents held that this was illegal as their founders had not held illegal religious tenets – and certainly not those held by nineteenth-century Unitarians. The only chapels that could be legally owned by Unitarians were those formed after 1813.

Disputes in the courts had continued for 25 years on these points, and decisions had consistently gone against the Unitarians. What appeared to be a final decision by the courts came in the House of Lords in 1842, which reluctantly affirmed the legal principle that no trust could be used to benefit something that was illegal at the time it was set up. Matters came to a head early in 1844, when it seemed that, without legislation to the contrary, Unitarians could be removed from their trusteeship of the majority of the chapels that they occupied by further actions before the courts, citing the Law Lords decision. Sir Robert Peel's Tory administration, to the surprise of many, with the apparent aim of preventing further law suits brought a bill before Parliament in March 1844 to secure the Unitarians in their places of worship.

The course of events leading to the passing of the Bill has been widely written about (see *TUHS* 1994 and *Faith and Freedom*, Autumn 2014). Gladstone, a member of the Cabinet, played a key role in the controversy, Several commentators consider that this experience marked a key stage in the development of his views on the relationship of church and state. Gladstone later recalled that the measure in some ways 'heightened my churchmanship but depressed my church-and-statesmanship' (Bebbington, p. 61).

John Bowring, then an MP, estimated that Unitarians were probably the largest group among nonconformists sitting in the House of Commons in the 1840s. However this did not mean that the Bill would be passed, as its publication produced a storm of opposition, even though it was a government initiative. Gladstone was not seen early in 1844 as likely to be among its supporters, for in 1838 his first book, *The State in its Relation with the Church,* gained a reputation among dissenters as being generally against their interest. Gladstone had argued that the Church of England was a branch of the historic Church catholic and in consequence had primacy in its relations with the state. The state had among its duties the support of religious truth, as embodied in the Established Church, against religious error. This filled Unitarians almost with disgust on its publication, and while in the years that followed Gladstone modified his view, they were at one with the rest of dissent in regarding him with considerable distrust. There seemed no reason to suppose that Gladstone should see a basis to secure the future of Unitarians, any more than he would support the cause of any kind of dissenter.

He was, however, deeply interested in the 1844 Bill, considering its contents closely, discussing them with the leading protagonists, and reading widely in the background papers of the various legal actions which had taken place. It became known that his view was not finalised, and Unitarians pressed their case with him. He received a deputation of three leading Unitarians on 1 June 1844, and he concluded in writing to his wife, 'Today I have been busy chiefly about the Dissenters' Chapels Bill, then had a deputation of the Unitarians – somewhat horrid: but on the whole I think there is more justice with them than against them' (letter, quoted in Shannon, p.153). Whether it was the members of the deputation or their ideas that he regarded as horrid is not clear; but he was impressed by the case that they made.

In the debate on the Bill in the House of Commons on 6 June 1844 he spoke for 75 minutes, and it was recognised at the time that his speech was the significant contribution that secured its passing, by 307 votes to 117. R. L. Shiels, who spoke immediately after Gladstone, opened with the prescient comment: 'The champion of free trade will ere long become the advocate of the most unrestricted liberty of thought' (*Parliamentary Debates*, p. 188).

Writing in 1876 in the *Contemporary Review* on the stand that he had taken, Gladstone concluded:

> The Unitarians appealed to Parliament. They showed that their
> Puritan forefathers had instructed them to discard all intermediate
> authorities; and to interpret Scripture for themselves, to the best
> of their ability. It would indeed have been intolerable if those, who
> taught the rejection of such authority when it was ancient and
> widely spread, should in their own persons, have reconstituted
> it, all recent and raw, as a bond upon conscience. The Unitarians
> concluded that they had obeyed the lesson they were taught, and
> that it was not their fault if the result of their fidelity was that they
> differed from their teachers.

Gladstone thus affirmed the individual's right to appeal to Scripture even if the theological conclusions reached were very different from his own or those of the Church of England. This was an important stage in the evolution of his own religious thinking on religious liberty.

The next stage

Gladstone's revised position was not due to his accepting Unitarian theological views. In reviewing a life of *Joseph Blanco White, the Spanish theological writer and priest who when in Britain had adopted Unitarian views, he wrote in the *Quarterly Review* (June 1845) of 'the freezing systems of Unitarian worship', adding in rather purple prose that White 'exulted in Unitarianism, as a starving garrison make a banquet upon a supply of garbage'.

Despite his activity on their behalf, Unitarians expressed pleasure at his resignation from office over the Maynooth grant (government support for a theological college in Ireland) in 1845. The *Christian Reformer* (March 1845), recalling his comments in his book *The State and its Relations with the Church*, commented: 'we rejoice that he is no longer a Minister of the Crown ... had it been permitted to us to judge of him merely by his conduct to ourselves, there are few indeed amongst the statesmen of the day to whom we should accord a higher place.'

However, if Gladstone's Christian orthodoxy was unchanging, his attitude towards people and their principles was evolving into something less rigid. His membership and attendance at meetings of the Metaphysical Society meant contact with figures from a broad spectrum of thought, religious and otherwise. This Society provided a significant forum for discussion among some of the leading thinkers of the day. Ranging in religious position from the Roman Catholic Cardinal Manning to the Unitarian James Martineau, the Society helped Gladstone to work towards an integration of his thought and a more open view. It was at meetings of this Society, for example, that he probably first met Martineau.

By the 1860s his position had moved significantly, as is demonstrated in his letter (2 January 1865) to **Samuel D. Darbishire**, a long-established friend and a Unitarian. He still held to his unswerving personal religious position, but he could take a more tolerant view of the stands taken by others.

I am sorry to say that I have not yet been able to read Mr Martineau's sermon, which I mean to do with care; and I am as you know one

> *altogether attached to dogma, which I believe to be the skeleton which*
> *carries the flesh, the blood, the life, of the blessed thing we call the*
> *Christian Religion, but I do not believe that God's tender mercies are*
> *restricted to a small portion of the human family ... I admit that there*
> *are schools of Christians who think otherwise. I was myself brought up to*
> *think otherwise, and to believe that salvation depended absolutely upon*
> *the reception of a particular and a very narrow creed, but long long have*
> *I cast those weeds behind me.*

Gladstone admired certain Unitarian writers and theologians whose books are to be found in his personal library, now contained in St Deiniol's Library, Hawarden. One of these was **Rev. Theodore Parker** (1810–1858), a radical American Unitarian, at odds with his own denomination, whose books had influenced Martineau. Gladstone saw that Parker's writings 'have much in them that moves sympathy and admiration' (letter to Rev. Charles Voysey, 2 July 1876, quoted in Lathbury, p. 103).

*Frances Power Cobbe, a writer with close Unitarian associations, attended Gladstone's breakfast gatherings (when out of office, Gladstone invited a range of people to meet him, in order to assess representative new thought, religious or otherwise) and she met him on other occasions.

> Miss Cobbe used to relate the amusement with which she once
> listened at Lady Louisa Egerton's to a series of after-dinner
> imitations by Mr Gladstone (then in his first premiership) of
> distinguished preachers (over thirty, she thought). 'But Mr
> Gladstone,' she said, when he concluded, 'you have said nothing of
> my pastor.' 'And who is that?' 'Rev. James Martineau.' Mr Gladstone
> was silent for a moment, and then said deliberately, 'There is no
> doubt that Mr Martineau is the greatest of living thinkers.'
> (Carpenter, p. 413)

However, Gladstone's view of Unitarianism at this time was complex and variable. In theological terms his response to the novel *Robert Elsmere* by Mrs Humphrey Ward, whose main character was seen as expressing Unitarian thinking, was highly critical. He compared modern

Unitarianism 'to a tall tree scientifically prepared for the saw by the preliminary process, well known to woodcutters, of clearing away with the axe all the projecting roots, which as long as they remained rendered the final operation impossible. This first process leaves the tree standing in a very trim condition, much more mathematical in form, as it is more near a cylinder, than in its native state. The business of the saw, when the horse and the man arrive, is soon accomplished' (Lathbury, p. 75).

Figure 7. W. E. Gladstone on his Hawarden estate,
armed with an axe for his hobby of tree-felling
(Elliott and Fry; Wikimedia Commons)

Gladstone appears to have made a distinction between Unitarianism as a movement of thought and organisation, and individual holders of its tenets, whom he clearly saw in a different light. He needed cordial relations with a politician who was widely known as a Unitarian, **Joseph Chamberlain**, though it is unlikely that they discussed theology. The same is likely to have obtained with *Sir James Stansfeld (1820–1898), another member of his Cabinet with close Unitarian connections. The relationship with Chamberlain was businesslike, correct, cool, and formal – but hardly friendly.

The Contemporary Review

In 1876, the fruits of Gladstone's thinking during his time out of office were contained in an article that he wrote in *The Contemporary Review* in June 1876, entitled 'The Courses of Religious Thought'. In his survey he did not reach beyond the borders of Christianity, as he did not regard 'instruction from the East' to be of current practical value. He saw these courses of thought as lying in five areas. Firstly the Ultramontane school, which accepts Papal authority; secondly the Historical school, which affirms the power of the Church but not the authority of the Pope; thirdly the Protestant Evangelical school, which rejects the first two but accepts the central dogmas of Christianity; fourthly the Theistic school, which rejects the dogmas but believes in a moral Governor of the Universe; and fifthly the Negative school, which rejects a moral governor and much else – a category which he considered includes eight sub-heads (scepticism, atheism, agnosticism, secularism, paganism, materialism, pantheism, and positivism).

The article produced considerable comment at the time, not least among Unitarians, whom he included in the fourth category or school. He argued that, while recognising one Almighty Governor of the World, they have come to their position by 'a declension from the Christian scheme'. Their leading figures may have a deep personal reverence for the Saviour; he quotes the example of Martineau. He then treats Unitarians specifically:

> Now we have no right whatever to impute bad faith to the
> profession of Unitarians and others, that they cannot and will not
> part with the name of Christians; that they are the true professors of
> a reformed Christianity ... Since the time of Belsham [the key early-
> nineteenth-century British Unitarian writer after Joseph Priestley]
> considerable changes seem to have taken place in the scheme of
> Unitarianism. At the present day it probably includes much variety
> of religious thought. But I am not aware that it has abandoned the
> claim to be the best representative of the primitive Gospel as it was
> delivered by Christ himself.

Individual thinkers have devotion and fervour still residing 'within this precinct of somewhat chill abstractions'. He lists excellent people in Britain and abroad who hold these views: 'I would pay a debt of honour to **Mr Martineau, *Mr Greg, *Dr Carpenter and *Mr Jevons**' (all of them leading Unitarians, two of whom were laymen, whose works he cites).

He fears that they will fail in their task, as their numerical weakness makes them 'an easy prey to the destroyer'. Their system is 'dry, abstract, unattractive, without a way to the general heart'. This statement seems to sum up Gladstone's view of Unitarianism in the 1870s, which is that its leading figures are worthy in many ways, but stark and chilly, commanding very limited support and attraction among the generality of people.

Attempts were made by Unitarians to challenge Gladstone's position, but he did not change his viewpoint. However, this *Contemporary Review* article shows the extent to which his position had moved, compared with his outpourings over his brother's marriage in 1835. His view of religious liberty had changed and evolved, and it was in this as much as anything else that his standpoint on Unitarianism had altered in the intervening period.

Gladstone appears to have summed up his mature view of Unitarians in 1874 in writing to ***Rev. G. Vance Smith** (BL MS 44443), a Unitarian scholar who controversially sat on the ecumenical committee in the 1870s that produced the Revised Version of the Bible in 1880. It is a generous and understanding statement, reflecting the width of his developed understanding; he states that he has had many friendships with

Unitarians, from which he has gained much. He is glad to acknowledge that God is not limited in how He operates, and that anyone who possesses the likeness of Christ is most truly His.

Sources

Bebbington, D., 1993, *Faith and Politics in Victorian Britain*, Grand Rapids USA.

British Library, Gladstone official papers.

Carpenter, J., 1905, *James Martineau.*

Checkland, S., 1971, *The Gladstones 1764–1852*, Cambridge.

The Christian Life, June 1876, January 1902.

Contemporary Review, November 1839, March 1845; June–November 1876.

Flintshire Record Office, Gladstone's papers.

Foot, M. R. D. (ed.), 1968, *The Gladstone Diaries*, Oxford.

Lathbury, D. C., 1910, *Correspondence on Church and Religion of W.E. Gladstone.*

Magnus, P., 1954, *Gladstone.*

Matthew, H. C., 1999, *Gladstone 1809–1898*, Oxford.

Quarterly Review, June 1845.

Ruston, A., 2008, 'The Chamberlains and Unitarianism', *TUHS*.

Shannon, R., 1982, *Gladstone, Vol 1. 1809–65.*

The Nineteenth Century, May 1888.

The Prime Minister's Papers, *WEG*, *Autobiographica*, ed. Brooke and Sorensen, HMSO, 1971, Vol 1.

TUHS, 1994, articles on the 150th anniversary of the Dissenters' Chapels Act.

Ward, W. R., 1973, *Religion and Society in England 1790–1850.*

From *Transactions of the Unitarian Historical Society*, 2008

7 The Lawrence family: nineteenth-century Unitarian Forsytes?

Those privileged to be present at a family festival of the Forsytes have seen that charming and instructive sight – an upper-middle-class family in full plumage. But whosoever of these favoured persons has possessed the gift of psychological analysis (a talent without monetary value and properly ignored by the Forsytes) has witnessed a spectacle, not only delightful in itself, but illustrative of an obscure human problem. In plainer words, he has gleaned from a gathering of this family ... evidence of that mysterious concrete tenacity which renders a family so formidable a unit in society, so clear a reproduction of society in miniature. He has been admitted to a vision of the dim roads of social progress, has understood something of patriarchal life, of the swarming of savage hordes, of the rise and fall of nations.

(J. Galsworthy, Man of Property, 1906)

The parallels between the Lawrence family (first of Hackney, then of south and west London) and Galsworthy's fictional Forsytes are remarkable. It is almost as if the author had known of the history of the Lawrence family written by ***Alexander Gordon** and adapted it for his purposes.

Both were families of the rising upper-middle-class, originating in each case from a dynamic founder of humble west-country origins. Both prospered from the enormous expansion of London in the mid-nineteenth century, which made them rich. In family terms, both argued incessantly among themselves and were kept together by spinster relatives. Both were conscious of the power that they derived from their large resources. However, they differed in what they did with that power. Galsworthy paints the Forsytes as being uninvolved in politics, religion, or social issues, concerned only with power inside their family and its immediate environs. The real-life Lawrences, on the other hand, very conscious of the power that their wealth gave them, were intensely involved from the very start in politics, religion, and society, and often to the exclusion of everything else. Their leading members had strongly held views on nearly everything, and they used their very powerful social position and financial clout to put their convictions into effect.

The Lawrence family

Virtually all the descendants of **William Lawrence** (1789–1855) were Unitarians, but the name is not well known, even to historians of nineteenth-century Unitarianism. This is maybe due to their active support of the older style of Bible-based Unitarianism which disappeared with the new century, but also because they had almost ceased to exist as a family unit by 1918. **Alfred** (1826–1875) had five children, all raised as Unitarian, but the rest of his many brothers and sisters only produced one child. The six members of this next generation of Lawrences again had only one child between them. Entirely London-based, they were not really part of the nexus of nonconformist families which, for example, is associated with the cotton manufacturers of Lancashire. This article attempts, first, to illustrate the unique role that they played in the Unitarianism of their time, showing how they used their benevolence to support a particular theological viewpoint, and, secondly, to evaluate their legacy to the movement in the twentieth century.

Up from Cornwall

William Lawrence was born in St. Agnes, Cornwall, the son of a tin miner, who decided very early in life to become a carpenter. He was clearly a young man of drive and ability:

> In 1808 he left St Agnes with two guineas in his pocket and a bag of tools on his back, accompanied by two young friends employed in the same handicraft. They worked their way to Plymouth and

thence took ship for London. Their first important piece of work
was the making of square balusters for a staircase, for which
they were each paid £5, accompanied with the offer of a second
engagement on the same terms. Lawrence's two companions would
take up no fresh work until they had disposed of the cash in hand,
while William at once seized the further opportunity and engaged a
couple of men as his assistants.

(Gordon, p. 6)

From then on he never looked back, setting up as a builder on his own
account in 1813 in Hoxton. By 1815 he had offices in Bread Street in
the City of London. The migration of his home and family is a record
of fast upward social mobility: from their home in Bread Street above
the office, they moved to live in Hoxton, then in Brixton, and by 1848
in Bloomsbury, in Tavistock Square. The year 1848 was the summit of
William's achievements, for he was elected Master of the Carpenters'
Company (having been a Freeman since 1815), Alderman of the City of
London, and President of the British and Foreign Unitarian Association.
He was involved in local politics from his earliest years in London, as
a member of the Parish Vestry (the local authority for the area at that
time) at St. Leonard's Shoreditch for many years. He consistently took the
liberal stand, and, according to his son's accounts in *The Christian Life* late
in the century, he was clearly not a man to be crossed. *Boase's Biographical
Dictionary* describes him as 'a Unitarian and a great reformer'.

William Lawrence came to Unitarianism via the Freethinking
Christians, a small closely knit sect founded by Samuel Thomason in
1798, which Lawrence joined in about 1815. Also known as the Church of
God, they rejected doctrines of the Trinity, baptism, and the Eucharist, and
the customs of public singing and prayer and the payment of preachers.
They met for Bible reading, addresses, and discussion. They maintained
the authority of the Bible, and their public antagonism to *The Age of Reason*
by *Thomas Paine gained them the name, which they did not repudiate,
of Freethinking Christians. This stand on the centrality and importance
of the Bible was an important influence on Lawrence and his children for
the rest of the century.

The Freethinking Christians were strongly opposed to the legal requirement that marriages must be solemnised in parish churches, and it was this affirmation that first brought William Lawrence into contact with Unitarians, who held similar if generally less strident views. He married **Jane Clarke** at St. Mildred's, Bread Street, on 21 September 1817 – but not without protest, an account of which he sent to the *Monthly Repository* which appeared in October 1817 as a letter arguing for civil marriage:

> *I enclose you a copy of a protest which was publicly delivered by the two parties: every effort was besides made by them to resist the performance of the ceremony, particularly by them refusing to kneel while the idolatrous and unchristian rite was performed.*

Besides the written protest handed to the incumbent, the congregation at various points in the ceremony uttered the words 'We protest'.

The move to Unitarianism

It is clear that after his marriage William Lawrence grew away from the restricted confines of the Freethinking Christians and towards the Unitarianism exemplified by **Rev. Robert Aspland** at the New Gravel Pit Chapel in Hackney. Here in the 1820s he met the famous, the learned, and the rich – whose company he found most attractive. Unitarian principles, once adopted, were never dropped or hidden: 'indeed his attachment to them seemed to increase with the advancing years ... he never shrank from the open avowal of his religious sentiments' (Gordon, p.17). He and his family were successively members of the Unitarian chapels at the New Gravel Pit Hackney, Carter Lane in the City, Essex Street off the Strand, and Rosslyn Hill in Hampstead.

William advocated what can be termed the Unitarian programme of the time, whatever the cost and risk of alienating the strong and powerful. Both before and after the passing of the Reform Act in 1832, which changed national political representation, he was spokesman at deputations to reassure King William IV that a national revolution was not about to take place. He refused to implement the harsher parts of the Poor Law Amendment Act in 1834 at Shoreditch, despite being ordered to do so, and with his sons he directly lobbied MPs and Peers in order to secure the passing of the Dissenters' Chapels Bill in 1844.

He was involved in everything and could be very generous with the large sums of money that he made from his building company, which was creating parts of the fast-growing suburbs. While many in the City of London regarded his politics as suspect, the force of his personality, his devotion to City institutions and charities, and his financial largesse meant that he could not be denied the highest of offices. He was elected Sheriff of London in 1849, appointing **Rev. David Davison**, a Unitarian minister, as his Chaplain. It was the first occasion on which a nonconformist had been so appointed. His chief aim was to become Lord Mayor, which would have occurred in 1857 had he lived. However, his sons more than made up for this deficiency.

The next generation

William and Jane Lawrence had ten children, all of whom, again like the fictional Forsytes, are buried in the family mausoleum at a big London cemetery (Kensal Green). It was the first and second sons, **William** (1818–1897) and **James Clarke** (1820–1897), and the youngest, **Edwin** (1837–1914), who became well known. **Alfred** (1826–1875) produced the only famous figure of the next generation: **Frederick William Lawrence* (1871–1961), who later became Lord Pethick-Lawrence, a supporter of women's suffrage and the last Secretary of State for India in the post-war Labour Cabinet, 1945–47.

All the nineteenth-century Lawrences were strong supporters of both the London District Unitarian Society (LDUS) and the B&FUA. William the elder was President at the inception of the LDUS in 1850, and his sons followed him into that office. Edwin alone refused the role of President of the B&FUA. There was hardly a time when a Lawrence was not to be found on the Council of either body. They were loyal supporters of **Rev. Robert Spears** and his traditional version of Unitarian thinking (see below):

Figure 8. Lord Pethick-Lawrence, British Secretary of State for India,
with Mahatma Gandhi, Delhi, 18 April 1946
(Wikimedia Commons)

their money always backed him and those who followed a Bible-based Unitarianism.

Their energy was remarkable. They worked hard in the family firm of William Lawrence and Sons until 1880, when they decided that they had made enough money and handed over the going concern, with capital, to their employees as a free gift: an almost unique example of benevolence, which received wide attention. But their main love was civic affairs, and after that Parliament. William and James each became an Alderman of the City of London, then Sheriff, and finally Lord Mayor in 1863 and 1868 respectively. William chose *Rev. **Thomas Madge** as his Chaplain, again the first nonconformist minister to be so appointed. James was Mayor when Queen Victoria opened Holborn Viaduct, so he immediately received a baronetcy. William was knighted and was to have been given a baronetcy, but this was prevented by his death. It was given instead to his younger brother Edwin, who had changed his name in 1898 to Durning-Lawrence after his marriage, emphasising the linkage with another well-known Unitarian family. Each of the three were Liberal MPs: William for the City of London, 1865–1885; James for Lambeth, 1868–1885; and Edwin for Truro, 1895–1906. The obituary for the latter in *The Times* on 22 April 1914 stated: 'In the Commons he did not play a very prominent part and it is said that his chief distinction in that assembly was that he wore the most expensive silk hats of any man in the House, their cost being, it is said, £30 each.'

The record of a father and two sons serving as Sheriffs of London remains unequalled. They were a close-knit family, the elder brothers being looked after by their sisters. Alfred's wife, Edith, is said to have found the argument and rivalry that regularly took place at family gatherings very daunting. Lord Pethick-Lawrence recalls what it was like in his autobiography:

> *My mother (a grand-daughter of Rev. Robert Aspland) was a very gentle woman who loved peace and harmony. She was frankly overpowered by the vigorous Lawrence personality, which enjoyed disputation and revelled in defending cherished beliefs. When she was left a widow at the age of 36 she had little or no experience of the world, and deferred without protest to the views of her Lawrence relatives. I came very close to her at many times in my life, particularly when I was alone with her, but when all her children were gathered round the table together, each expressing an opinion in a loud voice, I think she wistfully regretted that there was so much Lawrence in us.*
> (*Fate Has Been Kind*, p.13)

This article does not list their numerous activities, or examine Edwin's notoriety as the energetic proponent of the idea that Francis Bacon was the author of Shakespeare's plays, a subject on which he wrote extensively. Like seemingly everything else that the family did, Edwin's standpoint cannot be said to be balanced, but as 'the Lawrences are one of the largest holders of real estate in the City of London' (*Times*, 22 April 1914), they could ignore the views of their critics. They followed the same pattern within Unitarianism – particularly James and Edwin, whose loud assertiveness at religious gatherings was renowned.

Unitarian witness

The flavour of the assertive Lawrence nature can be gathered from the application to Eton College made on behalf of young Frederick (Pethick) Lawrence by his guardian, the redoubtable Uncle Edwin:

> *When my uncle decided (1885) I was to go to Eton, he looked out*
> *for the best of the masters and was recommended to H. E. Luxmore.*
> *Arrangements were nearly complete when my uncle mentioned that we*
> *were Unitarians. At this Mr. Luxmore said he would rather not take me,*
> *for though he was not bigoted, my presence would cramp his style when*
> *giving religious talks. As a result I went to another house.*
> (*Fate Has Been Kind*, p. 14)

William, the eldest of the three brothers, took part in numerous Unitarian activities, and his name headed many subscription lists. However, his was a quieter presence, which was perhaps just as well, as James and Edwin attempted to stamp their views and personalities on Unitarianism in all its manifestations. **Rev. T. L. Marshall**, author of James's obituary in *The Inquirer*, 29 May 1897, neatly summed up this attitude:

> A Unitarian, not merely by descent, but by thorough, strong,
> intelligent conviction, there was scarcely a denominational
> institution with which he was not more closely connected ...
> Sir James throughout his career belonged to the essentially
> conservative school of Unitarianism, and in our various internal
> controversies expressed his views with characteristic energy and
> ability. It may be doubted whether he always fully appreciated the
> thoroughly religious spirit of those who held a somewhat different
> form of Unitarianism from his own, but he never made a personal

enemy ... Some may remember the warm tribute he paid at a
Council meeting of the B&FUA to the memory of Dr. Crosskey, who
had been one of his most vigorous opponents in more than one
memorable controversy.

These were generous words from the magnanimous Marshall. James,
whose main platform for over thirty years was the LDUS, which he founded
in 1850 with his friends, strongly attacked Marshall's editorship of *The
Inquirer* in the 1860s on theological grounds and wanted to set up a rival
paper. This happened later when *__Robert Spears__, who had been brought to
London in 1861 by James as a missionary, set up *The Christian Life* in 1876
with Lawrence money. Sir James even provided the paper's title.

James was associated with a large number of Unitarian bodies. He
exerted his influence through them, and on London Unitarianism in
particular, from the 1850s to the 1890s. His views (he was an irrepressible
public speaker, but refused to preach) became very well known, and with
his brother Edwin he used his financial power to back them up. 'Few were
the occasions when money was required for Chapel buildings, whether
new erections or improvements, when Sir James did not come forward in
aid' (Gordon, p. 35). The references to the Lawrences in *The Christian Life*
are legion. At the end of his life a letter from James, read at the National
Conference at Sheffield in 1897, encapsulated his standpoint:

> *I intended very strongly to urge the absolute necessity of keeping to the
> faith and not wavering, and that the deepening of the spiritual life of our
> churches could not be furthered by mere philosophic speculations, which
> fail to touch the heart or conscience.*
> (*CL*, 10 April 1897)

Edwin was even blunter, as the following example illustrates. The
Lawrences had played a significant role in the building of Essex Hall
off the Strand in London and of Essex Church in Notting Hill Gate, in
both of which they maintained a proprietorial interest: not for them the
disinterested approach. In 1888 part of Essex Hall was let commercially to
the Ethical Society for meetings. Edwin (*CL*, 17 November 1888) stormed :

The practical suggestion I offer to all who, like myself, object to being tarred, is to do the same as I have resolved, viz, not to contribute one penny to any lectures or any other meetings held at Essex Hall so long as the Ethical Society is permitted to use any part of it. Last year Miss J. Durning Smith [his future wife] and I each gave £25 to the Education Committee. This year we will give nothing until the home of Unitarian Christianity is purged.

Essex Hall and Essex Church

Controversial though the two brothers were, their role in endowing the new Unitarian headquarters in 1887 is perhaps their most significant achievement. By 1880 the congregation founded by Theophilus Lindsey, meeting in Essex Street off the Strand, found itself in an area of declining population, with its supporters moving out to the suburbs. Closure was under consideration, the issue being complicated by the need of the B&FUA, the Sunday School Association, and other Unitarian bodies to move out of their rented premises in 37 Norfolk Street, Strand, to somewhere nearby. The idea was for the B&FUA to move to Essex Street and for the congregation to go to Notting Hill. The Charity Commissioners objected on technical grounds, but some clever thinking solved the problem.

The congregation would move to Notting Hill, taking over the Iron Church in the Mall, which had already been built and endowed by Sir James. The B&FUA would buy the Essex Hall site and build anew, following an appeal. These transactions were made possible by funds and loans given at crucial times by the Lawrence family, who also provided significant sums of money towards the building of the new Essex Church in what is now Palace Gardens Terrace. It can be said that the Unitarian movement in the twentieth century was able to have its permanent central site in London because of the vision and commitment of the Lawrences. No. 1 Essex Street was purchased and donated by Frederick Nettlefold, and this building later became (in 1916) Lawrence House, where Unitarians could stay while visiting London, as it was converted and equipped through their gift. Both buildings were destroyed in World War II, and the Lawrence House Fund is today the only memorial to their name; it enables younger Unitarians and those who have served in HM Forces to attend meetings and events.

The ubiquitous Edwin

Edwin Durning-Lawrence and his wife Edith were active everywhere after he left Parliament. His character was delightfully recalled by *Professor Dorothy Tarrant in 1967 at a dinner of the London Unitarian Club; the text of her tribute was subsequently published as a pamphlet:

> *He was a great and generous man and loved to run regular parties for Unitarian Sunday Schools at his country home near Ascot. A bluff, hearty sort of man, proud of all he possessed, especially of his excellent physique. I remember he once came to speak to Mr Ion Pritchard, who was a quiet little man. Sir Edwin stood over him and talked about the good health he enjoyed. He looked at Mr Pritchard and said. 'Have you got your own teeth?' and received the reply 'Yes, I've paid for them.'*

Apart from the key role that he played in founding the London Unitarian Club in 1903, Edwin's most significant involvement was with the Unitarian Home Missionary College Manchester (later Unitarian College). The settlement of the College at Summerville in Daisy Bank Road, Manchester, was 'largely due to his support' (McLachlan, pp. 99, 142–3). He was probably the College's chief financial backer, which was in large measure due to his personal support of the then Principal, Alexander Gordon, who later wrote the Lawrence family history. Edwin was President of the College from 1910 to 1912.

Social and theological initiatives gained his support, most of which were suggested by Robert Spears. Edwin and his wife created Durning Hall in the East End of London in 1889, which became a Unitarian centre for social work. **Rev. William Ellery Channing**, perhaps the most significant thinker and preacher in nineteenth-century American Unitarianism, greatly influenced the Lawrence family. Republishing his extensive works was an enthusiasm, Edith paying for the publication of 10,000 copies in the 1870s, and Edwin sponsoring the cheap centenary edition in 1880 in a massive printing of 40,000. He believed that the Unitarian name should be applied to chapels in the denomination and should be pressed at every opportunity. For example, he and *Sir John Brunner, the industrial magnate, supported the Unitarian Van Mission (an attempt in the early years of the twentieth century to spread Unitarian views by preaching throughout the country from the back of an adapted horse-drawn cart) by meeting the cost of the second van in 1906.

Figure 9. The Unitarian Van Mission
(Unitarian Historical Society)

At his death in 1914 eulogies appeared, as might be expected, in *The Christian Life,* which had indeed lost its most generous supporter. *The Inquirer* (25 April 1914) provides a more balanced view in a comprehensive obituary by **Rev. W. G. Tarrant**, its editor at various times:

He did not hesitate to assume a conspicuous share of whatever business was going on around him. He took sides heartily and the vigour of his expressions at times approached to vehemence. One would say that he was not careful to dress his opinions to suit those around him, he rather laid himself open on occasion to their amused regret, and it would not be candid to deny that the feeling of some passed beyond that state ... His juvenility, indeed, not only surprised, but at times perplexed his friends, what would he say and do next?

The eclipse

After World War I the Lawrence family took no active part in Unitarianism. Lord Pethick-Lawrence maintained a loose connection with it all his long life, mainly through his friendship with **Rev. Frederick Hankinson**, who first visited him in prison in 1916, where he was incarcerated as a result of his actions in support of women's suffrage. Before 1897, F. W. Lawrence (as he then was) financed and edited *The Christian Freeman*, a popular Unitarian monthly which appeared from 1859 to 1909. Surprisingly there was no obituary of him in the Unitarian press at his death in 1961.

His sister Annie J. Lawrence (1863–1953) built the unique piece of architecture at Letchworth in Hertfordshire known as The Cloisters. She was associated with the Unitarian group which met there in the 1920s, but there is no suggestion of a closer connection than this, although a Unitarian minister conducted her funeral.

The sole Lawrence who was a committed Unitarian in the second half of the twentieth century was **Theodora Durning-Lawrence** (1890–1971), the child of the late marriage of James Clarke (who was aged 70 when she was born). Later adopted by Edwin and his wife, she attended Essex Church all her life, and was its most consistent and generous financial supporter. Within a few years of her death, the building that had essentially been paid for by her father and uncle had been demolished and rebuilt. While always limited in her mental capacities, she left a large sum of money – but not to the benefit of Unitarianism. Her adoptive parents, conscious of her mental limitations, created trusts, called the Aston Charities, to fund organisations that they supported. In the Charities' now long existence, the support given to Unitarianism has been small.

Durning Hall (and the associated Lawrence Hall) was closed in 1950. What remains of the Lawrence legacy is tiny in comparison with their impact in the nineteenth century. However, their money and drive helped to provide Unitarianism with a newspaper, its denominational headquarters, and later the building occupied by the Unitarian College. Both of these latter organisations have had a significant influence on the movement's development since 1914, and the important part played by the Lawrences in fostering them deserves recognition.

Sources

The Christian Life, January and April 1897, April 1914, May 1926.

Contemporary Review, 1856.

Gordon, A., 1915, *The Lawrences of Cornwall Family History;* preface by Lady Edith Durning-Lawrence.

The Inquirer, February 1903.

McLachlan, H., 1915, *Unitarian College 1854–1914.*

Memorials of Robert Spears, Ulster, 1903.

V. Miles, 1967, *The Cloisters Letchworth.*

New Gravel Pit Chapel Account Book, Hackney Archives.

F.W. Pethick-Lawrence, 1941, *Fate Has Been Kind.*

M. Rowe, 1959, *Story of Essex Hall.*

A. Ruston, October 1987, *The Terrier* (Hackney Archives).

D. Tarrant, 1967, *Recollections of London Unitarians before World War 1.*

C. Titford, 1912, *History of Unity Church Islington.*

TUHS, 1969, 'Non-Con Club'.

From *Transactions of the Unitarian Historical Society,* 1992

8 Locked in combat: James Martineau and the Unitarian Association

Obituaries are one of the first sources that I consult when undertaking historical research: are there any obituaries that will help? I knew that those composed for James Martineau in 1900 must be numerous, in addition to those published in the Unitarian press. A laborious search in the British Library Newspaper Collection seemed to be in prospect – but this was not needed, as in the archives of Harris Manchester College they are all set out in a large handsome black leather volume, entitled *The Memorial Notices of Dr Martineau*. The original cuttings are glued on fine paper. They cover the period from 4 January 1900 to 17 January 1903, amounting to 118 published in Britain, the USA, and beyond; and they are indexed. In length they vary considerably, and their sources range from *The Times* and *The New York Times* to humble church calendars. It appears that his biographers hardly used them.

The obituaries provide those personal details that make James Martineau, ever (to me at least) a remote and austere figure, come alive. For example, the course of his typical day was recounted in *The Times* and the *Daily News*, 13 January 1900:

> Even when nearly 90 he rose at 6, worked three to four hours before a 1 p.m. lunch. Then a rest, a constitutional, and the newspapers in which he took a keen interest. His dinner hour was 5 p.m., and nothing would induce him to alter it. After dinner and a cup of tea he wrote and read until 12; then to bed to enjoy a child's sleep.

The Manchester Courier of 13 January 1900 brought out an obscure but illuminating fact, showing that, while filled with high thoughts, Martineau had, when it came to personal finances, his feet very much on the ground:

Dr Martineau insured his life for £1000 in 1828, and his executors are being paid £4331. It is not often that a life policy is in force for 72 years. However he would have done better if he had saved the premium on a regular basis which at compound interest at 3% would have amounted to £6000 and at 4% £9000.

Then we have his appearance, which was graphically described in the *Daily Chronicle* for 15 January 1900:

Dr Martineau's appearance was so striking that none who ever saw him could forget. The tall, spare form; the sad worn, deeply lined face, clean shaven but crowned with thick hair which did not whiten until an advanced age; the quick eager glance; the agile step; the look which told of sorrow and of profound thought; the clear, slow, emphatic utterance ... His speech was as unique as his style, the word fitting the thought with an exactitude which was wonderful.

Figure 10. James Martineau (1805–1900)
(Unitarian Historical Society)

How the correspondent knew that the word fitted the thought is unclear, but we can see what was meant. Many reports talk of Martineu's clear, slow, emphatic utterance. Much is revealed about the man that shows how his nature and personality were expressed in his actions and his writings. An example of his sense of humour, if that is what it was, comes from the *Eastern Daily Press* (15 January 1900):

> Sometimes Dr Martineau exhibited a sense of humour rather baffling to his antagonists, as, when Cardinal Newman piously observed that the only safeguard against German criticism was the shield of the spirit, Dr Martineau dryly retorted that another was ignorance of the German language.

These fascinating obituaries, often from the pens of people who had known him for many years, reveal not only his strengths but also his weaknesses. However, this present article centres on his involvement with organised Unitarianism, which was almost a love/hate relationship, as it was a topic that he could never seemingly leave alone. To set the scene, my final introductory quote is taken from the obituary in the *Daily Graphic* (15 January 1900), which aptly summed up Martineau's position in just two sentences:

> Dr Martineau was always a Unitarian, but he drew a distinction between a Unitarian and a Unitarian Church. The one you might be, he declared, the other you could never have.

The early years

Martineau began his career as a young minister in 1828. Until the late 1830s he was in essence a follower of the ideas of Joseph Priestley, who in the late eighteenth century laid down the theological and philosophical basis of Unitarian thought. These views, developed by Thomas Belsham, were followed by most Unitarians until the mid-nineteenth century.

He became increasingly unhappy with this Bible-based approach, which pervaded Unitarian thinking. But until the early 1840s he was a loyal and consistent supporter of the British and Foreign Unitarian Association, known almost universally as the Unitarian Association. He participated in its work (he preached its anniversary sermon in 1834) and clearly felt little problem in giving the body his support.

Two key events prompted the change in Martineau's position on organised Unitarianism. The B&FUA sponsored a special meeting in June 1838 with the object of bringing the whole body of Unitarians in Britain into closer and more effective union. During the debate Martineau raised a warning voice. He approved of the Association and would seek to defend it, but if its constitution became entirely sectarian, aimed at the diffusion of one fixed form of theology, it could not be regarded as realising the ideals and desires of the meeting. He was not sanguine about the success of any sectarian union or schemes of organisation.

By the mid-1840s Martineau admitted that his views about the validity of the constitution of the Association had changed. He stated that his eyes had been opened by the Lady Hewley case and its culmination (in 1844) in the passing of the Dissenters' Chapels Act, which brought out clearly the importance of the history and basis of the old English Presbyterian churches. (See Chapter 6 of this current volume.)

By expressing this change of view, Martineau began from the late 1840s to alarm most of the preachers and churches within Unitarianism by his preaching and writings. Their religious view was focused on the Bible and their traditional interpretation of its content. Martineau was a pioneer of the use of German Biblical scholarship, and his developing ideas of the importance of the enlightened conscience led to an alteration in his thinking.

This article does not seek to examine the impact of his altered viewpoint in the 1850s and early 1860s, and the clashes that these created between the different factions. However, an example from 1864 shows how far Martineau had travelled theologically, and the problems which the leaders of the denomination, some of whom were his College contemporaries and friends, had in keeping up with him.

The autobiography of *Moncure D. Conway (1832–1907), the secularist and leader of the South Place Ethical Society, would appear to be an unlikely source from which to find out about Martineau's thinking and theology. Although from opposite theological poles, Martineau and Conway were representative nineteenth-century religious figures. Conway became a convinced secularist, while Martineau often poured scorn on those who adopted an atheistic, or even agnostic, theological position. Conway had been an American Unitarian minister, and in the early 1860s he served South Place Chapel Finsbury, which was still nominally a Unitarian place of worship. He therefore took part in London Unitarian ministers' meetings at this time, and what follows is Conway's account of a gathering held on 26 October 1864 (*Autobiography*, p. 46).

> Mr Martineau opened the topic after tea: it was, how far the phrases
> applied to Christ in the New Testament, e.g. Lord, Saviour, Prince etc.,
> were really characteristic of Christ, and had any meaning for us now.
> It was the most powerful piece of theological statement I ever heard. He
> proved conclusively that these names all referred to the idea of a kingdom
> of Christ, begun after the alleged ascension. The great characteristic
> of modern theology was, he said, a shifting of the scene of Christ's
> power and influence from heaven to earth, from a future to history –
> consequently those phrases and titles have no religious meanings for us
> now. It was very sweeping ... I was the only one out of the fifteen present,
> I believe – certainly the only speaker – who heartily and entirely agreed
> with Martineau.

> I remember that in closing the discussion Martineau said he must
> decline to answer any of the arguments that had been adduced from
> consequences. The fact that the fallacious titles and phrases were used in
> their own Unitarian hymns and literature, and that all these might have
> to be expurgated, could not be weighed against the claim of truth and fact.

This last section shows Martineau at his most difficult, winding up his hearers with superb intellectual analysis, which was well received, followed by digs at what they were doing or preaching. When challenged, he often refused to respond, or evaded their concerns about the hornets' nest that he had stirred up. Martineau did not consider that he should, to use a modern phrase, 'win friends and influence people' among Unitarians. They must take the truths as he expressed them as they stood.

Rising denominational feeling

Martineau's dislike of denominationalism grew in the 1860s. It was expressed in his quest for the creation of a truly national, all-embracing church that would contain what he understood to be the catholic spirit of English Presbyterianism. In particular he saw no place for the B&FUA, which was increasing in effectiveness under the leadership of his old college friend, **Robert Brook Aspland**, who took an entirely different view of Unitarianism and its future development. Martineau did not, however, cease to be an individual member, and he was a regular attender at its meetings.

He took a bold initiative in 1868 by founding the Free Christian Union, which aimed to transcend the various Christian denominations. His inability to persuade and organise effectively was a major factor in its collapse in 1870. This was one of Martineau's big defeats, and a major disappointment in his long life. Few individuals and no churches joined the Union, and leading figures within every denomination, including Unitarians, studiously avoided it.

In the 1870s Martineau was therefore left with Unitarianism, and in particular the organised version provided by the B&FUA. Martineau's views had had no impact on church structures; his influence was on individual thought and spirituality among leading Christian thinkers through his hymn books, prayers, and teaching. He directed his energy again to make the Unitarian movement into his ideal national church. Increasingly he believed that a major obstacle to its creation was the continued existence of the B&FUA, which had expanded beyond the limited intentions of its founders. Aspland had died in 1869, and his deputy **Robert Spears** (1825–1899) took over as Secretary. Spears was an entirely different character from Aspland, and the scene was set for a clash.

Martineau and Spears were chalk and cheese. Spears came from a working-class background, with a strong Northumberland accent and little formal education, and he was twenty years younger than Martineau. Yet he had founded newspapers, and as a young minister revolutionised the position of old English Presbyterian congregations. He believed passionately in the Bible and the Unitarian interpretation of it. Spears (as Chapter 10 of this volume illustrates) was a man of enormous dynamism and a superb organiser. The clash between the two men was over what each saw as the heart of Unitarianism.

The Inquirer

The story of the dispute is set out in the columns of *The Inquirer* of the time. Researchers go to Martineau's voluminous works to ascertain his views, but *The Inquirer* is almost an equally informative source, enormous but more revealing of the man. Unfortunately it is not indexed. From the 1840s until the late 1880s *The Inquirer* is filled with Martineau, what he wrote, and reports of what he said. If they reported him wrongly, he was quick to tell them, to judge by his published letters. The readership must sometimes have tired of Martineau, despite his brilliance, for he was ever present, year in and year out. He used its columns as a means for presenting his religious thinking to the public; his opponents called *The Inquirer* a Martineau rag, though it was not a justifiable claim. In the early 1870s it was the only weekly national Unitarian newspaper, so what it printed was of significance.

Martineau wrote on most issues, be it about theology or organisation. One of his central continuing concerns was the need for improved payment of ministers, particularly in rural areas, which should be provided from a central source. This proposal cut across the deeply held congregational polity of Unitarian churches; it has never been adopted. He sometimes went into detail to describe how his vision of a reinvigorated English Presbyterianism should be created; this was side-stepped by Unitarians. To use a modern expression, Martineau was almost a control freak when it came to the Unitarian movement. He was determined to get his own way, and his manner of operation within Unitarianism was very different from the one that he adopted outside of it.

Essentially this is all brought out in the two key clashes between Martineau and the B&FUA which took place in 1872 and 1876.

No Unitarian churches

Martineau started out from the premise that a Unitarian Church *per se* was an impossibility. Writing to **Rev. S. K. McDonald** in 1859, he stated:

> *To make the Unitarian doctrine the essence of our church appears to me to imply, unless we surrender the whole idea of a church, a re-adoption of that very notion of* Orthodoxy *(as entering into the relation between God and man) which we profess to reject.*

(Martineau, 1894, Vol. 2, p.391)

The two long letters to McDonald, an obscure and not very successful Unitarian minister, arose out of a correspondence in *The Inquirer* (Martineau, 1894, Vol. 2). These set out Martineau's argument against organised Unitarianism, if that faith is to be true to itself. Moncure Conway again sums up Martineau's position (*Autobiography*, p. 47):

> Though a leader of Unitarians, he was not a leader of Unitarianism. He had in his mind an ideal English Church though for the moment it consisted of himself and his chapel. It was to gather under its wings all the religious minds, and make the nation a fountain of living waters for all races, without any doctrinal Christianization of them. He was jealous of everything that tended to detach the Unitarian spirit and critique from the general religious life of the country, or organise it into a distinct church. It was here that his contempt for 'consequences' had serious effects.

Who owns the building?

Spears quickly made the Unitarian Association into a publishing power house, producing cheap editions of the works of the American Unitarian **William Ellery Channing** in tens of thousands. Spears had invigorated London Unitarianism in the 1860s and he was now attempting to repeat the feat on a national scale. New and rich supporters on the B&FUA Council meant that Spears could do much, especially as the rich Lawrence family financially backed the majority of his projects. They believed that their variety of Bible-based Unitarianism was the faith of the future, and the word Unitarian must be proclaimed everywhere. Spears stated that there was 'no shilly-shallying with the word "Unitarian", which must be applied to every church or chapel' (*Memorials of Robert Spears*, p. 10). Compare this with a statement in Martineau's letter to *P. W. Clayden of 1865: 'the word Unitarian is exactly fitted for its purpose of theological distinction, and cannot yield other service, however cruelly you strain it on the rack' (quoted in Upton and Drummond, p. 419).

The B&FUA had suffered for many years from not having an adequate office base in central London from which its activities could be expanded. A series of rented addresses in the Strand area did not provide an adequate focus for the dissemination of the Unitarian approach. Spears and his supporters believed it was vitally important that the B&FUA find a permanent place, their own building, from which to launch the Unitarian triumph which was to come. **James Hopgood**, a rich supporter, offered to donate a large sum, around £20,000, towards the purchase of a building.

In October 1872 it was announced that the B&FUA was about to buy a building. Martineau intervened at once in *The Inquirer* in a series of letters (9, 16, and 23 November). While agreeing that it needed better quarters, he took the strongest objection to the Association becoming the owner of a permanent freehold estate, a building held in a closed trust for a Unitarian purpose. Martineau continued (9 November 1872):

Looking upon the Association itself as a temporary necessity, of recent origin, and doubtful duration, I think it would be a serious

mistake to provide for it as if destined to a perpetuity which
certainly its founders never contemplated. (A tenancy under
a lease) not bound by the terms of a trust, and free to comply
with the conditions of an unknown future (is needed) ... Such a
measure (purchase of a building) tending to the consolidation of
a 'Unitarian denomination' would be a formal renunciation of the
principle which has been our unique and honourable distinction ...

Were there to be a building in London, dedicated to an open trust,
to religion, philanthropy and educational objectives ... an adequate
proportion of it might be let or lent to the Unitarian Association
for its particular purposes.

The dispute went backwards and forwards, with suggestions being
made that Martineau was doubting the good intentions of the B&FUA's
Council. This he rebutted. James Hopgood wrote ably and at length to
explain why he wanted to give the money to make the project possible.
Martineau would have none of it: 'I protest that to endow this type of
opinion [the views of Priestley and Belsham] is as much against good
sense as to endow any other doctrine or truth like Free Will' (7 December
1872).

In his published responses Spears appeared evasive and he did not
handle the dispute well. By December the project was put on hold, and
it was decided not to accept Hopgood's offer; instead, when a new office
was taken, the Association would be a tenant in a building held on an
open trust. Resolutions on the subject pressed by Martineau continued
to be discussed in 1873.

This is exactly what happened in 1887, when Essex Hall was built
in Essex Street on the site of Essex Street Chapel, the congregation of
which had moved out to Notting Hill. The building was held on an open
trust for the purposes which Martineau had wanted, with the B&FUA
and other Unitarian bodies using it as their base at no cost. It was in the
governance of individual trustees and remains so to this day. Neither the
B&FUA nor its successor, the General Assembly of Unitarian and Free
Christian Churches, has ever owned its own office building.

Martineau's triumph was therefore permanent, but Moncure Conway (*Autobiography*, p. 47) regarded the incident as an odd 'consequence' of Martineau's thinking and the power that he exercised within Unitarianism:

> One occasion, when there was reported at the annual meeting of the Unitarian association a large bequest left it, Martineau declared that the money would tend to entrench in a sort of fortress a spiritual movement that should be perfectly free. The sectarian wing of the association was strong but the personality and moral genius of Martineau prevailed. I doubt whether in Christian history there can be found another instance of a religious association rejecting a large bequest of money.

Publishing that book

The second clash between Martineau and the B&FUA was over a trifling matter, but behind it lay far-reaching implications. The dispute demonstrated how widely the 'new' Unitarian thinking, prompted by Martineau and others, had taken over. Roger Thomas, writing in the *TUHS* in 1969 on the events of 1876, concluded that the resignation of Spears from the secretaryship of the Association meant that 'the pure doctrine of Biblical Unitarianism was dead'.

It must not be thought that members of the B&FUA Council were all adherents of the Bible-based Unitarianism that their secretary Spears advocated. Changes in membership in the 1870s shifted the balance toward those who saw much value in the new Unitarian ideas but still did not necessarily want to follow the direction advocated by Martineau. In 1875 this faction proposed that the B&FUA republish one of the key works by the American Unitarian **Theodore Parker**, entitled *A Discourse on Matters Pertaining to Religion* (first published in London in 1849). Its author had died in 1860, and the work had been reissued by a British commercial publisher in 1872 and 1873. There were plenty of copies available, and it was on sale in the B&FUA bookroom.

Why did the B&FUA need to republish? There was no reason to do so, except that it contained material hostile to the Bible-based Unitarianism that was followed in the USA, as it had been in Britain, in the 1840s. Parker accused Bible-based Unitarians of misusing the Bible and treating it as a tool for which it was not intended. He believed that 'Unitarians creep behind Biblical texts ... ready to believe anything with "Thus saith the Lord" before it, and explain away what is offensive ... the Scriptures in their hands are a piece of wax' (quoted in *The Inquirer* 4 March 1876).

The new faction won the day, and it was decided in January 1876 to republish Parker's work under the imprint of the B&FUA. Spears had successfully objected to a similar move in 1872, and this decision infuriated him and his associates. They argued that its publication would be inconsistent with the objects of the B&FUA. As *The Inquirer* was seen by some as a Martineau puppet, in the excitement of the time its reporter was denied entry to B&FUA meetings. Spears on his own initiative then issued a contentious paper which set the whole dispute alight. He stated that publication was a leap in the dark, which might involve a rupture within the Association, if not its ruin. It was an injustice to attack the Christian and Unitarian position with the funds of the Association, as *A Discourse* was 'a rude assault on Christianity and the Supernatural in religion'.

This set in train a variety of claims and counter claims, and specially convened meetings were held at short notice that were highly combative in tone and content, almost vituperative on occasion. Martineau stated that *A Discourse* was 'a noble book' and that he 'would always be prepared to resist any attack on Parker as he had done thirty years ago'. He poured scorn on what might or might not be published by the Association:

> It seemed to involve the principle that every peculiar phase of
> Unitarian thought ought to be represented in the literature of the
> Association. That was to say, that the Association was to provide a
> museum for the exhibition of all the eccentricities of thought and
> opinion, that all the diversities of thought and feeling were to be
> imported into the catalogue of their library, to show what a pretty
> sort of people they were.
> (*Inq*, 25 March 1876)

Martineau's admirers in the Church of England and elsewhere would have been surprised at the harsh tone that he sometimes adopted in these internal Unitarian disputes, but it was the religious world of his family, and as such did not come to the attention of his wider audience.

Spears' blast had not advanced his case. In March 1876 the B&FUA Council passed a compromise resolution, concluding that while it might well publish Parker's work in the future it would not do so at present, as there were sufficient copies available from other publishers. Spears regarded this as a prevarication and resigned. Although the implications were not clear at the time, this action marked the end of Bible-based Unitarianism as a force; the standpoint of Martineau and his supporters had won the day.

However, nobody really wanted Spears's resignation from the B&FUA secretaryship, such had been his dynamism, commitment, and level of achievement. A large subscription was raised in his support which kept him financially secure for the rest of his life. It was rare to see Martineau's name appearing on subscription lists, and this was not seemingly due to lack of money. However on this occasion even he gave five guineas for the support of his old rival. Spears immediately founded *The Christian Life*, a weekly Unitarian newspaper which he successfully edited for the rest of his life; it challenged *The Inquirer* and specifically much that Martineau stood for. Spears was scoring points off the Grand Old Man whenever he could, right up to the early 1890s.

Perhaps the best comment on the clash came from **Henry W. Bellows** (1814–1882), the leading American Unitarian minister, who supported Spears rather than Martineau. In the issue of *Liberal Christian* (New York) for May 1876, he wrote:

Robert Spears' hot earnestness for Unitarianism of the conservative school has served to make him an extraordinary worker ... Advanced Unitarians are too often blind to the fact that a large part of the work our body has to do is ... presenting common Christendom with the means of escaping from its bondage to old and hurtful errors.

Martineau triumphant?

In football terms that was 2–0 to Martineau. He had stopped the B&FUA holding its own property under the Unitarian name, and had effectively seen off that variety of Unitarianism with which he grew up: an amazing achievement in the religiously charged times of the 1870s.

But was it a triumph? Was he successful in the long term? In some ways yes, and in other ways no. His moral and religious influence and thinking were dominant in the late nineteenth century, but when it came to its reflection in organisational terms he was a complete failure. His advocacy of the term 'Free Christian' held sway in many places, but in others there was equal insistence on the use of the word 'Unitarian', and the clash went on for decades. When the emotion had died away, a compromise between the two perspectives was achieved in the 1920s with the creation of the General Assembly of Unitarian and Free Christian Churches. Formal Unitarian organisational structures can be said to have triumphed in the twentieth century. It is ironic that it was Martineau who was the first person to stress the need for a General Assembly within Unitarianism (in 1888 in an address to the National Conference at Leeds), but when it was created in 1928 the body was not constituted in the way that he would have wanted.

And the B&FUA? This 'temporary body with a future limited life', according to Martineau, carried on its work by appointing (successively after Spears) **Henry Ierson** and **W. Copeland Bowie** to the post of general secretary, and both were successful in expanding its scope and standing. The B&FUA became recognised nationally, both inside and outside Unitarianism, as the main representative body of the movement.

In 1915 the B&FUA became an incorporated body, so that it could hold land and property; this would have been to the horror of Martineau, as the Association was being given a permanent life – and the Unitarian name along with it. Nobody objected to what was generally seen as a sensible development. After the creation of the GA in 1928, the B&FUA was not abolished but expanded its role as the custodian trustee of chapels and funds, most of which had once been English Presbyterian. It thereby provided a permanent national Unitarian presence inside the trust deeds of churches and chapels. This role it continues to fulfil today.

Unitarianism had changed since Martineau's day and was no longer centred on the citation of Biblical texts as the chief justification of its beliefs. There was a general feeling that it was necessary to move away from the intense internal arguments of the nineteenth century, many of which centred on Martineau and his views. After the First World War the British religious scene was very different from that of the 1890s, and so was Unitarianism in Britain.

Sources

Conway, M., 1904, *Autobiography: Memories and Experiences*, Boston USA, Vol 2.

Inquirer April, November 1872; January and March to May 1876.

Martineau, J., 1888, *Essays, Reviews, Addresses.*

Martineau, J., 1894, *Suggestions on Church Organisation.*

Memorials of Robert Spears, Ulster, 1903.

Rowe, M., 1959, *The Story of Essex Hall.*

Ruston, A., 1999, *TUHS.*

Thomas, R., 1969, *TUHS.*

Upton, C. and J. Drummond, 1902, *Life & Letters of J Martineau*, Vols. 1 & 2.

From *Transactions of the Unitarian Historical Society*, 2002

9 The omnibus radical: Rev. Henry Solly

Mr. Solly is rather a peculiar man, and one of his peculiarities is that he believes that the whole human race are born to be hewers of wood and drawers of water for him in the promotion of objects of public utility. I warn you all, that unless you are prepared to sell yourself body and soul to Mr. Solly you will have a very bad time of it. For thirteen years I have been trying to defend myself from him and I have not been successful.
(Solly 1893, Vol. 2, p. 442)

These words, spoken by *Lord Lyttleton at a soireé in October 1874, describe a human dynamo of a man, entirely committed to the nineteenth-century idea of political and social reform. *Henry Solly (1813–1903) lived too long for the good of his reputation, and for much of the twentieth century he was a forgotten figure, appearing only as a footnote in various histories of nineteenth-century social movements. Although he was immersed in Unitarianism all his life, that movement has served him no better, except for a few generous comments made by R. V. Holt in the 1930s (Holt 1938, various references). However, there are signs that his importance is beginning to be recognised, and recently articles have appeared on Solly in several places (see Woodroofe 1975 and Williams 1987).

This article does not attempt a comprehensive evaluation but seeks to enumerate his varied activities, and plot his uneasy relationship with Unitarianism. He upset Unitarians in almost every sphere, and he knew it, but at the same time desperately wanted their recognition of both himself and his works – a recognition that he never achieved. Solly played a cantankerous but important role in nineteenth-century Unitarianism.

Henry Solly did not hide his light under a bushel. His two volumes of autobiography, published in 1893, are a mine of information. *These Eighty Years* shows signs of truncation, and there is no index. In a supportive review, *The Inquirer* did have to conclude that 'the reminiscences would have been better if they had been compressed into one volume, instead of being spread out into two closely printed volumes of more than a thousand pages'. Maurice is quoted in the preface that 'a man should be an artist to write a biography as much as to write a romance, and if Mr Solly had been more of an artist he would have observed the laws of proportion' (*Inq* 6 January 1894). Perhaps this is true, but it is difficult to ignore the size and range of the autobiography. It is necessary, however, to be careful not to take Solly at his own evaluation.

Personal background

Henry Solly's early years are covered extensively in Volume I of his autobiography, as well as in obituaries and other sources. He was born in London on 17 November 1813, descended from generations of nonconformists on both sides of his family. His father, **Isaac Solly** (1769–1853), was a descendant of *Daniel Neal, the Puritan historian, and a leading director of several companies. He came to grief in the financial crisis of 1837, a factor which influenced Henry's later life. Isaac's father took a major part in the erection of the Presbyterian meeting house in Walthamstow in 1730. It was in this area, at Leyton House, that Henry spent his early years, attending the school of the Meeting's minister Rev. Eliezer Cogan. The family was connected with the Unitarian movement at this time but adhered closely to the English Presbyterian name. Solly puts over this point clearly in his autobiography (Vol I, p. 54), as well as providing a foretaste of his later views on the position of servants:

> One circumstance connected with the Old Meeting Walthamstow which struck me as a child with some amount of wonder took place whenever our carriage was required to convey us to 'meeting' (never Chapel). For at the conclusion of the hymn following the sermon, the coachman and footman, who sat in the gallery, always got up and went out (missing the last prayer and benediction) to get the horses and carriage ready so that the master and mistress might not have to wait. Some audacious questionings, I believe, which however I scarcely dared to propound openly, arose in my mind as to the relative importance of religion to the coachman and footman compared with their 'betters' ... My grandfather

*and grandmother Solly had an extreme dislike, as I have heard my
father say, to the name 'Unitarian': and though my father and mother
were somewhat reconciled to it by their friendship and esteem for Dr.
Priestley, they would never have tolerated for a moment the Old Meeting
in Marsh Street Walthamstow being called a Unitarian Chapel.*

Later he attended the school of the Unitarian minister at Brighton, *Dr
John Morell, before proceeding to the new University College, London in
1829. On the completion of his studies, his father wished him to enter
business. Henry tried commercial life for some years, but it was not to his
taste. When his father faced financial ruin in 1837, Henry decided that he
needed to look elsewhere for his life's work. On the advice of **Rev. Robert
Aspland**, who considered that Henry had sufficient formal education to
become a Unitarian minister, in 1840 he spent a brief time at the General
Baptist Academy under Rev. Benjamin Mardon. Never fully at home in
the mainstream of Unitarianism, in later life he always found the General
Baptist Assembly more to his theological liking.

His career in the Unitarian ministry began in 1840 at Yeovil, where he
stayed until 1842. His subsequent ministries were at Tavistock (1842–44),
Shepton Mallet (1844–47), Cheltenham (1847–51) Carter Lane, London
(1852–57) and Lancaster (1858–62). None of his ministries was long; most
were ill paid and were troubled by social and theological differences with
leading members of the congregation. At the end of his London ministry
in 1857 he concluded:

*On the whole, I could not help feeling that my London pastorate, and
work there generally, had been rather a failure, and the back of my life at
five and forty seemed broken.*
(Solly 1893, Vol. 2, p. 140)

Unable to find an appropriate pulpit, he launched in 1862 into new
fields, when he founded the Working Men's Club and Institute Union.
From then on he became involved in a great variety of activities, mainly
associated with the social condition of the working class, at which he
worked unceasingly until the late 1880s.

Living in London, at Hampstead, he never received a regular salary or stipend again. His income derived from various paid secretary posts or editorships which came and went, and he was often in a precarious financial position. He wrote copiously from the 1850s onwards: plays, articles, and booklets on social and religious issues. A full list could not possibly be assembled today. Most, however, were of transitory interest.

In 1841 he married **Rebecca Shaen** (1812–1893), daughter of Samuel, of the Unitarian family from Crix in Essex. They had five children, his son **Henry Shaen Solly** becoming the minister of various Unitarian chapels. His eldest daughter, **Emily Solly**, married *Rev. P. H. Wicksteed in 1868, a Unitarian minister but known as a Dante scholar and leading economist of the period. Soon after his wife's death in 1893, Henry Solly went to live with his daughter Emily and son-in-law. He died at their home at Childrey, near Wantage, on 27 February 1903. He was buried at Childrey, and his grandson, **Rev. J. H. Wicksteed**, yet another Unitarian minister, conducted the service.

There was a brief notice of his life in *The Times* (5 March 1903), but not in other national newspapers or journals, apart from those connected with Unitarianism and his former spheres of activity. I wrote his entry for the *Dictionary of National Biography Missing Persons* Volume which appeared in 1993, an entry which was largely repeated in the *Oxford DNB*. Solly is difficult to classify: the only epithet that could easily be applied to him is 'Victorian reformer and social innovator'.

Social activist and reformer

Between the 1840s and the 1880s Henry Solly was involved in nearly every radical movement that in any way affected the social condition of the working class. His name often appears as a footnote in social histories of the period. This article does not provide a full record of his activities, but most have been mentioned. Religion played a vital part in his life and work, as his autobiography reveals. Religion and social activism constitute two complementary sides of his personality, a factor that he recognised in 1862 when he left Lancaster for London and what was in effect his new career:

Here I was, at last, going up to London once more, in greater loneliness than ever, and filled rather more, I am afraid, with doubts and fears, than with thankfulness and hope: yet amid all these conflicting feelings, with a sense of escaping from a prison into the free air, where there would, at least, be room to use my own wings. But I felt assured of one thing – that I was not giving up my deliberately chosen profession of the Christian ministry, and that I should still be working for my Master as decidedly (and perhaps more effectively) as if I had continued to be the minister of a regular Christian congregation.

(Solly 1893, Vol. 2, p. 201)

*Lord Beveridge, in his seminal work, *Voluntary Action*, has a section on Solly which concludes (p. 170): 'He was a restless, inventive, constructive spirit, part author of at least three large living movements: working men's clubs, charity organisation and garden cities.'

Working men's clubs

The first of these movements, the Working Men's Club and Institute Union, was probably his greatest achievement and lasting memorial. Founded chiefly at the initiative of Solly on 14 June 1862 at an inaugural meeting held in Waterloo Place, London, there are today nearly 4,000 clubs with many thousands of members. Solly left Lancaster to become the Union's first paid secretary in the autumn of 1863, at a salary of £200 per annum. Since the 1840s he had been a strong supporter of clubs and institutes for working men, places where they could meet together socially, for mutual improvement, and where tea and coffee were plentifully available but no alcohol. In Solly's view, intemperance was one of the greatest diseases of the age.

All his energy was put into the new Union, and he proved to be excellent at fund raising and getting support from the rich and powerful. In addition to this London activity, he went round the country setting up working men's clubs virtually by the force of his personality. His single-minded commitment to the task was summed up very well in his obituary notice in *The Inquirer* (10 March 1903, p. 150):

How that society throve, adding to its ranks many of the leading reformers of that strenuous period, and how it developed in one direction after another, always receiving the zealous and passionate service of its secretary, is a history well worthy of the 19th century. Mr. Solly's name became widely known and everywhere with respect, and genuine admiration was mingled with the gentle satire of sayings like Henry Fawcett's 'Here is Henry Solly, who thinks heaven will be composed of Working Men's Clubs'.

However, the Clubs refused to develop in ways that Solly wanted. Many sold alcohol as a means to expand, and not all wanted to discuss the socially elevating subjects that their founder required. That, however, was not the only problem. Terry Williams describes what happened next:

> In 1867 Solly's flamboyant style, extravagance and continual demand for more money became too much for the other members of the council and he was forced to step down. He took his dismissal badly, and on the instigation of the Duke of Argyll he formed a rival society, 'The Social Working Men's Club Association', which, after some early success due mainly to the noble patronage, soon fell into decline and by 1871 Solly was back at the Union. No sooner was he reinstated as secretary than the two honorary secretaries resigned, and with good reason. With Solly back in the driving seat the Union had to start paying wages again. His stay this time was short, and by early 1873 he'd left, never to hold office again.
>
> (*Inq*, 14 February 1987)

But the Union never forgot its debt to Solly. It was fully represented at his funeral, and the then secretary, writing in 1904, concluded:

> If the work which the Clubs do, if their influence on personal character and their contribution to the sum total of human happiness be correctly appreciated ... then shall the investigator reckon Henry Solly amongst the constructive statesmen of our time.
>
> (Solly 1904, p. 214)

Charity organisation

The second area to which Lord Beveridge believed Solly made a significant contribution was charity organisation. His time in this area was brief, but his contribution was signal and very well documented. (See Mowat 1961, Bosanquet 1914, and Jones 1971.)

Solly, believing that the Working Men's Clubs catered for the industrious artisans, looked round for a related field of endeavour and turned his attention in 1868 to the submerged criminal element. Using his now excellent contacts with the aristocracy, he managed to set up a lecture, under the auspices of the Society of Arts, with the Bishop of London in the chair, to consider the issue. He concluded that there was no one better qualified to lecture than himself, which he did on 23 June 1868 under the title *How to Deal with the Unemployed Poor of London and with the 'Roughs' and Criminal Classes*. Helen Bosanquet (1914) observed:

> There is no doubt that Mr. Solly's paper gave the trumpet call which summoned the forces into the field. It resulted immediately in committees of influential men, who formed themselves into an association and issued a series of prospectuses.

From this lecture and by a series of complex negotiations, mainly conducted by Solly, arose the Charity Organisation Society in 1869. This became a key body involved in administering charity and relief in London in later years. By the 1940s it had become a family case-work agency. It has been argued that it was this body that first introduced and developed social case-work techniques in this country. For a few months leading up to its foundation, Henry Solly was the organising secretary and presiding genius. But yet again he was forced out – this time more quickly, yet, it would appear, for similar reasons that led to his departure from the Union. Solly quotes them himself in his autobiography (Vol. 2, p. 355):

> *The position of affairs in relation to myself came out pretty clearly one day at some meeting in the office we occupied in James' Street in the Adelphi, when Captain Maxse said in his frank, seaman-like way, 'Some of you complain at Mr. Solly because he always wants his own way. Of course*

he does. So does every man who wants to get an important work carried
on and thinks he knows how it is to be done. And then some other persons
say he only wants to make a comfortable berth for himself. But had that
been his object he would have tried to ingratiate himself with everyone of
us, instead of that he has opposed each of us in turn all round.'

This was another instance where Solly made a key innovation in an area
of social concern. As with the Union, the organisation that he helped to
create soon passed out of his hands, leaving doubts and uncertainties not
only about his role but also concerning his personality.

Garden cities

The third area mentioned by Lord Beveridge was what were termed
'industrial villages'. In 1884 Solly read a paper before the usual distinguished
audience that he seemed to have a genius for assembling, entitled *Home
Colonisation. Rehousing of the Industrial Classes, or Village Communities v.
Town Rookeries.* The aim was to alleviate overcrowding in towns, prevent
rural desolation, and relieve destitution and poverty generally. He suggested
setting up new village communities, containing their own industries and
means of livelihood, and also their own social centres. As ever, Solly set
up an organisation to promote his ideas, this one entitled The Society for
the Promotion of Industrial Villages. It soon disappeared, for a variety of
reasons, and now at the age of 71 Solly had had enough:

This Society was the last of my forlorn attempts to promote social reforms
by means of an organised association and I mean it to be the last, for
which probably those friends who have often helped me, and those whom I
have also worried but who have not helped me, will be devoutly thankful.
(Solly 1893, Vol. 2, p. 566)

In this effort Solly predated the work of Ebenezer Howard and the Garden
City movement which he created following the publication of his *Tomorrow:
A Peaceful Path to Reform* (1898). The concepts of William Morris and
the various ideal, classless communities set up in the 1890s would not
have appealed to the very practical Solly. He was a firm believer in the

class system, his dream of social regeneration being based on improved fellowship of class with class. Solly, despite his father's financial failure and his own often impoverished condition, always regarded himself as a gentleman, a member of the established order and certainly a cut above the social status of a dissenting minister. His industrial villages, however, though not revolutionary, were a novel idea in the 1880s, and have been considered an important precursor to the work of Howard.

Temperance, Chartism, and Co-operation
To see the work of Henry Solly in terms of these three areas alone would be a misrepresentation. His other involvements (they could not be given the lukewarm title of 'interests') include his life-long opposition to alcohol and its abuses. He occupied positions in the temperance movement before it was fashionable, and wherever he was living. His support for the main radical social movements in the 1840s has been referred to in several works; at the time of his death his work a full sixty years before had not been forgotten. He was one of the two ministers of religion who attended the Birmingham Chartist Conference of 1842 as a representative (of the Yeovil Chartists). His autobiography has been used as a source for early Chartist history. (Chartism, a radical reform movement demanding change, was thought by many in the 1840s to be the start of the British political revolution.) His connection with Chartism was an experience that he never forgot. It was the subject of his most successful novel, *James Woodford, Carpenter and Chartist*, but the connection alienated the leading rich Unitarians of his day and was one of the main causes of their distrust of him.

Solly was associated with the co-operative movement and is listed as one of the main supporters of the first of the modern Co-operative Congresses in 1869 (Brown, p. 51). He also helped to establish the Society at Lancaster in the 1850s. In a related area, as early as 1846 he held meetings at Shepton Mallet aimed at obtaining the early closing of shops *(Inq* 1846, p.749). Solly pressed for the opening of museums, libraries, etc. on Sundays to provide 'illumination and instruction' for the working class in particular. He thus became a founder member of the Sunday Society and was a Vice-President for many years.

Journalism and adult education

He rarely entered the political forum directly, but he has a place in the history of the British Labour movement in that he was the editor of the *Beehive*, which became the chief organ of organised labour of its time. The trade union leader and journalist *George Potter (1832–93), long associated with the *Beehive*, appears to have been as difficult as Solly. His entry in the *Dictionary of Labour Biography* states:

> In August 1869 Potter helped to establish the Labour Representation League, which forthwith adopted the Beehive as its organ. Potter's old opponents, still to some extent distrusting him, then manoevered Rev Henry Solly into the editorial chair, with Potter as joint editor. But Solly's informing and elevating journalism satisfied few of the London Trades Union leaders and he gave up the editorship at the end of 1870.

This is not the way Solly saw the matter; he believed that he had made the journal 'hum'. 'For my own part I liked the work immensely and had all my life longed to engage in it. But it came to an untimely end ... the difficulty of working with a colleague, who I found afterwards had, from the first, disapproved of my being added to the staff, was complicated by a fundamental difference on the subject of Temperance' (Solly 1893, Vol. 2, p. 385).

Solly also got involved in education for the working classes. He formed the 'Trade Guild of Learning' in 1873, which Lord Beveridge saw as 'the germ of adult education classes of a vocational cast'. He soon resigned from this as well, for the usual range of reasons, and he followed this up with the founding of the Artisans' Institute. This institution combined a liberal and a technical education, and Solly with his usual energy provided much of the former. Lord Beveridge points out that this preceded the foundation of the City and Guilds Institute, whose work is still of importance today, and Solly claimed that his organisation helped to form the pattern for this Institute. The indefatigable man also made an input into the Working Men's College, founded in the 1850s by Rev. F. D. Maurice. Solly was a great admirer of Maurice, the celebrated Anglican thinker who was the son of a Unitarian minister, and he shared many of his theological and social presuppositions.

All these activities were on the grand scale, but Solly's reformist and caring zeal also went out to humbler causes. I will end this section with an example quoted by him that was undoubtedly representative of the man.

> *My frequent journeys to and fro on the Hampstead omnibuses made me acquainted with several grievances under which the men were unjustly suffering, and which I tried to remove ... I went to the Police office to speak for a man summoned for loitering ... The magistrate dismissed the summons stating that a place must be provided for drivers to wait between journeys. Nothing however was done in consequence, so I went to Scotland Yard, interviewed one of the Commissioners of Police, and in ten minutes the whole difficulty was settled, by leave being given for the Hampstead omnibuses to wait in a vacant place by St. Giles' Church where they rested undisturbed for several years.*
> (Solly 1893, Vol. 2, p. 340)

Errant Unitarian

Henry Solly's grandson, **Rev. Joseph Wicksteed**, wrote an appreciation of his grandfather as a preface to the reissue of *Working Men's Social Clubs* in 1904. It is an affectionate but telling recollection of the old man, whom he had known since boyhood. Brought up a Unitarian, Wicksteed expected in his youth that his grandfather would share his views. He got a nasty shock:

> *I was talking, doubtless a little boastfully, of my Unitarian ancestry, and it was a new thing in my life to hear from him that this name, so full of associations to me with all the people and impressions that I most loved, was not the name under which he wished to stand ... But as further discussion evoked, there was more than a name at issue between us ... I was filled with anxious and fruitless perplexity for many a day. For some years after this, religion was a forbidden subject between us ... Unfortunately, however, my grandmother was unable to reconcile herself to his departure from the line of growth so precious to herself.*

Yet although Solly denied the title Unitarian, affirming instead his attachment to the English Presbyterian name and latterly to the more Biblically based General Baptist tradition, he never formally left the Unitarian ministry. His autobiography (Vol. 2, p. 504) shows that 'Unitarian minister' was the title that he accepted to the end of his days:

Another friend of the Club movement had previously begged me to drop the ministerial title as he thought it impaired my usefulness and success. Perhaps this was so, especially as I found afterwards that when it was asked what denomination I belonged to, the answer often seems to have been he is a Unitarian minister.

For all the years when he lived at Hampstead, he was a member of Rosslyn Hill Chapel and attended whenever he could. Unitarians were his constant companions, both as family and friends, although Unitarianism seemed to move farther away from him in its religious thinking. The obituary in *The Christian Life* put it appropriately:

Though grouped with Unitarians, Mr. Solly's views were really more correctly to be described as Arian, and he endeavoured at all times to bridge the chasm between orthodox and heterodox and had friends in both camps.

Yet even on the subject of his dislike of the Unitarian name he was inconsistent. As minister of Carter Lane Chapel, he was asked to join the committee of the B&FUA. He refused, because 'I still felt strongly the objections to the controversial and inadequate name of Unitarian, to which Jews and Mahometans had as much right as ourselves' (Solly 1893, Vol. 2, p. 96). But he then went and joined the propagandist and assertive London District Unitarian Society, formed in the 1850s, and toured missionary stations delivering addresses such as 'The Origin of Unitarian Christianity in this Country, and the Right Blessing of Free Enquiry' (LDUS Annual Report, 1856).

Solly always seemed to take the role of irritant and sought to oppose those in positions of power. He identified himself with those who sought to challenge the status quo. In Unitarianism this was the 'Top Ten' people or families in congregations and districts – a phrase that he regularly uses in his autobiography. Often he seems to have set out to be difficult from the start. He took, for example, a strong stand against American slavery, and because many leading Unitarians in the USA held the same view in the 1840s and 1850s, he thought that British Unitarians should all be as committed as himself. When they showed that they were not, he exploded in print. The following is not an untypical example of his blasts:

> The estimable men who object to the introduction of the subject at the approaching meeting of the B&FUA evidently view it, not as a Church fellowship, but as a business meeting, terminating in a pleasant convivial reunion of sympathising friends. If they had just seen their sister sold at the auction block, or their mother groaning under the cow-hide, they would more readily rejoice at a church meeting which in the name of Christ might protest against the foulest system of villany ever practised in God's sight since Christ died to redeem us.
>
> (*Inq*,7 June 1851)

He attacked every view that seemed to be leading English Presbyterian congregations into organised Unitarianism, even doubting the benefits of the Dissenters' Chapels Act, which was so universally admired among Unitarians:

> Had the Bill not passed there would have been such a manifestation of religious life and zeal among the Presbyterian descendants of the ejected ministers as England had not witnessed since the days of Wesley ... was that [the Bill] but a mere sordid struggle to keep possession of a few endowments?
>
> (Solly 1859)

James Martineau's Free Christian Union (1869) attracted Solly, and he took a leading part in its formation, although he was not surprised when it failed. Solly, Martineau, and Maurice were very much on the same wavelength – although not politically, for Martineau was staunchly Conservative. Martineau wrote to Solly (4 February 1861): 'What we must strenuously resist, is the tying up of chapels, funds, constitutions – all that belongs to the future – by doctrinal exclusions.'

While he could be seen as almost a Unitarian leper, at the same time Solly sought acceptance by both men and women – in whose rights he was a great believer. For most of his life Solly was to be found at Unitarian meetings, or those of the General Baptist Assembly. He wanted to follow his father by being appointed to key Unitarian organisations and charities, but that was not to be.

Solly's grandson, Joseph H Wicksteed, evaluated his life in the following terms, which might help us to understand this complex individual, forceful and irascible, but essentially a man of simple faith:

> *Life was real to him. not as being the expression of something more real behind, but with all the vivid intensity that the tangible world of things has to a child. Life was to him a great and wonderful romance, but because this world was his own. Its joys and pains were his ... To him, wrongs and suffering were not symptoms of false ideas among men at large, but definite evils to be fought with and removed now and on the spot.*
>
> (H. Shaen Solly, 1904, p. 9)

Sources

Beveridge, W., 1948, *Voluntary Action.*

Bosanquet, H., 1914, *Social Work in London 1869–1912*, London.

Brown, W. H., 1928, *A Century of London Co-operation.*

Holt, R. V., 1938, *The Unitarian Contribution to Social Progress.*

Jones, G. S., 1971, *Outcast London*, Oxford.

Malchow, H. L., 1983, *Agitators in the Age of Gladstone and Disraeli: British Pressure Groups 1865–1886.*

Mowat, C. L., 1961, *The Charity Organisation Society, 1869–1913*, London.

Oxford DNB.

Solly, H., 1859, *Our English Presbyterian Forefathers.*

Solly, H., 1884, *Home Colonisation: Re-housing of the Industrial Classes; or Village Communities v. Town Rookeries*, pamphlet, London.

Solly, H., 1893, *These Eighty Years*, 2 vols. (St Deinol's Library, Hawarden, holds a copy of this work, closely annotated by W. E. Gladstone, which Solly had sent to him).

Solly, H.Shaen, 1904, *Working Men's Social Clubs*, second edition, Preface.

Strange, D. C., 1964, *British Unitarians Against American Slavery*.

Williams, T., 1987, on Solly, *Inquirer* 14 February 1987.

Woodroofe, K., 1975, 'The Irascible Mr Solly', *Social Science Review*.

Obituaries in Unitarian journals.

From *Transactions of the Unitarian Historical Society*, 1988

10 Robert Spears: the nineteenth-century Unitarian dynamo

To speak adequately of Robert Spears would be to give a history of Unitarianism in these islands for about the last half century, so involved has he been in every question affecting our denomination.

These words, uttered in March 1899 by **Rev. S. C. Pinkerton** (*CL*, 11 March 1899), accurately reflect the life and work of a notable man. They appear in an obituary following the death of *Robert Spears at his home in Highgate on 25 February 1899. He was one of the most remarkable figures to adorn Unitarianism in the second half of the century, at a time when vivid personalities abounded. To many inside and outside the movement, Spears was seen as the representative Unitarian figure.

Figure 11. Robert Spears (1825–1899)
(Unitarian Historical Society)

118

Robert Spears was largely uneducated and was proud of his humble beginnings at Lemington, near Newcastle upon Tyne. He retained a broad Northumbrian accent all his life, despite many decades of living in London. He significantly expanded the membership of every congregation to which he ministered, and he helped to create new causes throughout the country. As well as founding newspapers, he was from 1867 to 1876 a dynamic secretary of the British and Foreign Unitarian Association. Yet today he is a largely forgotten figure, probably because many of the causes that he espoused did not accord with the religious, and particularly Unitarian, zeitgeist of the late nineteenth and early twentieth centuries.

Robert Spears made a signal contribution to the development of Unitarianism in the second half of the nineteenth century. He was a powerhouse of energy, devoted to his traditional Bible-based version of Unitarianism, for which he campaigned incessantly, refusing to accept objections or obstacles. He wrote and published extensively for decades. His continuing legacy is Channing School, now a girls' private school named after his hero, **William Ellery Channing**, which he helped to found in Highgate in 1885. However it was Spears' vision, taken up by others, that was a major contributing factor in the expansion of the movement between the 1860s and the 1880s.

Spears did more to gather in new Unitarians and build churches than did the competing witness of **James Martineau** and his supporters, with their emphasis on 'Free' Christianity and their aversion to the application of the term 'Unitarian' to anything but individuals. Spears' message was direct, and he attacked head-on anything that he considered to be vague:

> *I call a spade a spade ... I have had, thank God, in a forty year ministry, distinctly named in every place 'Unitarian', a measure of success it may be useful for persons who are timid about the word 'Unitarian' to know. In 1851 I was pastor of our church in Sunderland. There was a mere handful of people, less than a score when I went: so few that the two or three could not be always got together. I had no stipend and so supported myself by a school. After seven years I left some 120 worshippers and had saved the property from being sold. Sunderland was much more intolerant towards*

> Unitarianism in 1851 than now. I did something there to soften the harsh
> tone of the orthodox, without abandoning the Unitarian name.
>
> (*CL*, 31 October 1891)

How did a young man of 26, arriving in Sunderland afire with the
Unitarian Biblical gospel in his first ministry, come to reach this position
of certainty?

Early years

Robert Spears was born at Lemington, a small village then about five miles
west of Newcastle upon Tyne, on 25 September 1825. He was the fifth son
of the eight children of John (1765–1849) and Mary, née Glenn (1783–
1874). John Spears worked as a foreman in an iron foundry. His religious
background was Scottish Presbyterian, and his wife was a Methodist.

Robert's formal education was very limited, and he started work as an
apprentice to an engineering smith. Self-taught, he was from an early age
much more interested in books, in which he was encouraged by his mother.
He quickly discovered an aptitude for teaching, founding a school when hardly
out of his teens. By 1846 he had joined the New Connexion Methodists at
Scotswood-on-Tyne and was soon a local preacher on trial. However, the basis
of his future heterodoxy had been laid in 1845, when he attended a debate at
Newcastle between Rev. William Cooke (1806–1884) of the New Connexion
and *Rev. **Joseph Barker** (1806–1875), who had been expelled from that
denomination and was at the time associated with the Unitarians. Spears later
claimed that it was this debate which made him a heretic.

The young preacher was soon in trouble with the Methodists. His
examination to become a fully qualified local preacher was the cause:

> He declared that he was perfectly willing to answer all questions, on
> the condition that they were couched in the language of scripture.
> and not taken simply from books explanatory of the Methodist
> beliefs, which were only, he said, the handwork of men. To the
> question 'Do you believe in the Trinity and unity of God?' he replied

that before he could answer the question it must be expressed as the New Testament expresses it ... The result of answers such as these was many meetings between Mr Spears and the leaders of his church, with, however, no satisfactory result. Whilst his mind was still in a state of suspense with regard to religious beliefs, Rev. George Harris (1794–1859), Unitarian minister at Newcastle, came to deliver a lecture [in 1849] at nearby Blaydon. Here we reach a turning point in his career.

(UUCA, 1903)

*George Harris was an eloquent and forceful speaker, and Spears was electrified: 'Mr. Harris's answers to my questions showed that I must change my religious home.' He continued to teach for the New Connexion, but was soon preaching for local Unitarian congregations, firstly in a little mission room at Eighton Banks. Spears came to believe that the Bible was Unitarian from beginning to end, and his admiration for the New Testament in particular became his passion for the rest of his life.

Unitarian ministry

In 1852, untrained except for some instruction from Harris, Spears began his ministry at the almost defunct Unitarian chapel in Sunderland. His success, repeated later in several other places, was rewarded in 1856 with his appointment to serve the Unitarian congregation, founded as English Presbyterian in 1688, at Stockton-on-Tees.

The congregation had been let down and ... could offer only £65 a year as a stipend. ... When I entered Stockton I recollect the dilapidated state of the pews and floor etc. as well as the small congregation. I avowed in that old Presbyterian building my Unitarianism and preached it with a distinctness never before known there, and at the end of three years left a renovated building and a congregation that filled the pews. The Town Hall was engaged for a gathering to bid me farewell. ... Two large meetings at Sunderland and Stockton were gathered to bid me good-bye,

*but in no case have I had a meeting to welcome me to any pulpit, for the
simple reason that such a meeting could not be got together. But in every
case where I left, such a welcome was given to my successor.*
(*CL*, 31 October 1891)

In December 1859 his surplus energy was engaged in founding a weekly
newspaper, the *Stockton Gazette,* based on the principles of Liberalism and
Free Trade. It became a daily paper later in the century, entitled *The North
Eastern Gazette,* which in the 1890s had a circulation of 40,000.

Migration to London

Spears' reputation and dynamism had spread among the Bible-based
Unitarians, who believed they had found a new champion who would
proclaim their beliefs from the housetops and in any place that would
provide him with an audience. The main proponent of this viewpoint
within Unitarianism was **Rev. Robert Brook Aspland** (1805–1869), who
brought Spears' work to the attention of **James Clarke Lawrence** of the
London District Unitarian Society. Spears was appointed to the ministry
of Stamford Street Chapel, in south London, in 1861.

This was a big challenge for an uneducated, unpolished, and little-
known minister whose experience had been confined to the north-east
of England: to revive a decayed urban congregation at the behest of a
Unitarian grandee who had assured him of a stipend of £100 per annum.
Such a task would have been beyond most people, but Spears made an
impact at once which set him on his life's work.

He steered the same course as before in proclaiming Unitarianism
and the Bible:

*In my ministrations there [at Stamford Street] I made open profession,
exposition, and defence of Unitarianism; and in seven years we had one
of the largest Unitarian congregations in London, and were freed from all
external aid. There was no dilly dallying about the name Unitarian.*
(*CL*, 31 October 1891)

It all went so well that in 1867 Spears was appointed co-secretary, with Rev. R. Brook Aspland, of the B&FUA, and in 1870 after Aspland's death he was appointed to the post of general secretary. A rise to such power and influence within Unitarianism only twenty years after joining the movement was unparalleled; his thrust and single-minded purpose had become widely recognised.

The few years that I had the honour of that office the income from all sources was nearly quadrupled. My aim was to make it £6000 a year, and this would have been accomplished ... The sale of books and tracts of the Association, during my secretaryship rose from £10 to upwards of £500 a year.
(CL, 31 October 1891)

Brook Aspland raised the B&FUA to a greater importance and representative position than it had previously enjoyed. However it was Spears, with the newer members of its Council, who took it to a new prominence in the 1870s, particularly through increased activity throughout Britain and in the number of books and pamphlets published. The B&FUA became recognised as being at the centre of denominational life and new enterprise. Even *The Inquirer*, ever critical of the B&FUA, had to admit in 1874:

> ... of late years the Association has been gradually emerging from its old position of a London Society, and assuming the National importance which it is entitled to claim. Its missionary activities have been widely extended ... and its publications have been on a bolder and more extensive footing.

Spears' activity on the national and international scenes did not mean that he neglected Unitarian expansion in London. With helpers that he always seemed able to recruit, he opened new causes at Forest Hill, Croydon, Peckham, Clerkenwell, and Notting Hill, all named Unitarian Christian Churches. This was of course in direct opposition to the views of James Martineau and his supporters, to whom calling a church Unitarian was an anathema. But even Martineau, almost in a different world from that of Spears, admitted that under him the Association had at last begun to merit the full distinction of its bold and ambitious title. No longer simply British, it had won the right to use the word Foreign as well, for Spears had expanded its role outside the British Isles.

Beyond Britain

Spears consistently sought to establish relationships with any person or group of people who seemed to be seeking the simple religion exemplified by the Jesus Christ whom he saw in the New Testament, even when they were not specifically Christian. For example, he established close contact with liberal religious movements in India, encouraging their representatives to visit Britain by setting up speaking engagements for them.

He justified this contact with others who did not share his specific view, believing that they would aid the dissemination of the Unitarian view of Jesus which he believed would ultimately triumph. 'My deeper respect for the Indian Theist is based on his deeper respect and love for Christ than the English Theist.' Spears' approach was evangelical, in that it owed much to his Methodist background. He was on the watch for indications anywhere of a greater willingness to follow 'the Great Master of Pure Religion'. He believed that 'it is not our differences which separate us in life, so much as the way we handle them' (*CL*, 25 March 1899). Spears applied this view to other branches of Christianity in Britain and Europe. It was his initiative in 1881 that helped to create the Sion College Conferences, a nineteenth-century attempt to foster ecumenical understanding which brought together different Christian opinions aimed at finding common ground.

Wherever Unitarianism was attempting to reach a new audience or place, Spears set out to be its friend and supporter. Two examples are to be found in *The Christian Life* of 11 March 1899, after his death. The first is in the form of a letter from **Ferdinando Bracciforte** of Milan, expressing 'the debt of gratitude which Italian Unitarian Christians owe to his memory'.

The second is on a more personal level, written by **Caroline A. Soule**, the pioneering American Universalist minister, whose missionary efforts were chiefly pursued in Scotland:

> *I remember very vividly the first time I ever met Mr Spears in May*
> *1875. I had come to the Old World a worn and weary worker, an invalid*
> *indeed. Very lonely did I feel as I found the way from my hotel to the*
> *Strand, for there was not a familiar face in all England. Shyly, and*
> *with a sinking heart did I enter the office of the British & Foreign with*
> *my letter of introduction. Never, never shall I forget the warmth of Mr*
> *Spears' greeting, that cordial grasp of the hand, those hearty words of*
> *welcome! I feel it, I hear them yet! ... during the weary six months of*
> *invalidism that followed, he never once lost sight of me, but followed my*
> *wanderings carefully, and in every possible way made himself a most*
> *useful and devoted friend.*

The turning point of 1876

Spears had undoubtedly energised the B&FUA, maintaining and developing the Bible-based Unitarianism of Aspland, in opposition to James Martineau and the transcendentalist and revolutionary ideas of **Theodore Parker**. During Spears' tenure as secretary of the B&FUA, the divergence between the theological factions within the movement became more marked. Martineau saw Spears as an orchestrator of sectarian 'bluster', and the 'New School' of thinking was gaining ground (*Oxford DNB*). The dispute with Martineau (described in Chapter 8 of this book) led to Spears' resignation on a point of principle.

> *It is better to keep a clear conscience than fill any office, however*
> *honourable and useful, if the hand has to perform what is contrary to*
> *the feelings of the heart. I am not without hope that my bitter opponents*
> *will live long enough to feel that they have neither served the interests of*
> *Unitarian Christianity, nor the public good in their zeal against myself.*
> (*CL*, 18 March 1876)

Spears now sought a new career in religious journalism.

Back into journalism

One of the 'cankers' within Unitarianism identified by Spears and his supporters from as far back as the late 1850s was *The Inquirer*. They believed that this, the only weekly Unitarian journal, had sold out to the Martineau camp and presented a most unsatisfactory view of Unitarianism, vague and without the key Biblical principles. Spears had been a professional journalist, albeit combining this employment with a ministry, so with the financial backing of the Lawrence family he was determined to become an editor again in support of the religious position that he held so dear. He had established *The Christian Freeman* in 1856, which presented simple messages each month to Unitarians. In May 1876 the first edition of the weekly *Christian Life* appeared. This journal was to be Spears' mouthpiece for the rest of his life.

It soon gained a circulation and offered a lively and intelligent alternative to *The Inquirer*, concentrating on reporting news from the churches. It attracted contributors who shared the editor's theological standpoint. These included the Egyptologist and translator of the Bible, *Samuel Sharpe**, and the historian of nonconformity, **Alexander Gordon**, who wrote regularly for the journal for decades. Spears ensured that an expansionary theme was constantly present in the columns of *The Christian Life*. The periodical continued to be published until 1929, when it merged with *The Inquirer*; the old theological disputes had by then lost much of their power. *The Christian Life* is a major source for those researching the Unitarian movement in the late nineteenth century and is perhaps Robert Spears' most enduring memorial.

A flavour of the combative line which Spears took in the early days of *The Christian Life* can be gathered from an extract from his review of a book by W. E. Gladstone on religion, which mentioned Unitarianism:

> ... the writers and speakers whom he is quoting may be such of us as do not acknowledge their belonging to the Unitarian sect.

Some of our ministers, while acknowledging Unitarian opinions, have said they were not Unitarian Ministers, that the Chapels in which they worshipped were not Unitarian Chapels, that their congregations were not Unitarian congregations, and that the College in which our Unitarian Ministers are educated is not a Unitarian College. ... The Unitarian sect may be divided into, first, those who are glad to own their Unitarianism; and secondly, those who for the most part avoid doing so.

(*CL*, 5 August 1876)

Spears constantly used the word Unitarian, with a capital U, and calling the movement a sect was apparently designed to annoy those who followed Martineau.

In 1876 Spears also produced what has proved to be his most significant book, and the most solid: *Record of Unitarian Worthies,* prefaced by a historical sketch of the rise and progress of 'the Unitarian Christian Doctrine in Modern Times, London, 1876'. The preface was 48 pages long, followed by a Unitarian calendar, and 384 tightly packed pages presenting the lives of prominent Unitarians. As the title suggests, the content approaches hagiography, and the persecution suffered by some is very fully covered. However there is much solid material, some relying on personal information not to be found elsewhere, and the book is a valuable research tool. In 1906 the B&FUA published an abridged version entitled *Memorable Unitarians,* containing short selected biographies, which had a wide circulation.

What Spears regarded as his key publication, first put together in the 1850s and brought out in numerous editions, can only be regarded today as a curiosity of its time. It was entitled *A Unitarian Handbook of Scriptural Illustrations and Exposition;* published latterly by the B&FUA. Fourteen thousand had already been printed by the time the 1883 edition was published. The first ten chapters are stated in the preface 'to contain a clear and simple statement, in the very words of scripture, of the belief of Christian Unitarians. ... The second part of this work is devoted to an exposition of almost the whole of the texts adduced by Trinitarians in support of their leading tenets.'

This is typical of Spears on what he regarded as his strongest ground: arguing and citing from Biblical texts. It is difficult to summarise the hundred dense pages, which consist almost entirely of annotated Biblical texts: it is today almost an unreadable book. To illustrate the nature of its content, part of page 6 is set out below, but without the wording of each text:

Unitarians believe OF CHRIST AND HIS DIVINE MISSION John vi 69, Luke i.79. Acts 10 ii,22, Titus ii,14. OF THE HOLY SPIRIT, OR INFLUENCE OF GOD: Luke xi, 13; 1Cor ii,12, John xv, 26.

New ministry

One poor area in east London in which Spears founded a new church was Stepney. From the early 1860s he had taken the lead and was soon organising some 200 adults and 400 children to receive religious instruction with a Unitarian slant in that part of London. In 1874 he decided to leave the ministry of Stamford Street Chapel and devote at least some of his energies to the creation of the church at Stepney, later named College Chapel. He delighted in the Sunday School work which he carried out for many decades in various places:

Probably the most successful of all my Sunday School work was that at Stepney, for which two considerable rooms had to be raised, one on top of the chapel and the other by the side of it, costing nearly £2000. I can remember 450 children attending this school, with 40 teachers, and we branched off to the east and founded a school in Limehouse, now Elsa Street; and a school at Cambridge Road, now Mansford Street, Bethnal Green. ... At our monthly social meeting held at Stepney, some 80 teachers usually sat down to tea. ... We did a little missionary work also. We opened the Limehouse Mission, now one of the most successful of our London Domestic Missions, where nearly 400 people, young and old, assemble every Saturday night and Sunday, and whose savings reach annually over £2000.
(UUCA 1903, pp. 11, 33–34)

In 1885 he moved his home to Highgate, to be near Channing House School for the daughters of Unitarian families (he had four daughters of school age), founded in the following year in association with Matilda Sharpe, one of his chief supporters at Stamford Street Chapel. She was the prime mover, but the choice of the name of Channing was due to Spears. The school continues to this day as a private non-residential school for girls in the locality, with a limited Unitarian involvement. He now directed his energies towards founding a church in Highgate, as there was no Unitarian place of worship near enough for the pupils to attend. This effort, combined with the weekly production of *The Christian Life,* taxed his energy and his robust good health for the first time.

Highgate Unitarian Church was soon on a firm footing. A hall was erected on Highgate Hill in 1885, and a church was added to it in 1890 which continued to serve the area until 1961. As in other places, Spears created a chapel library open to the public; it was the only free library in the area until 1906. The local authority commenced building the North Library in Manor Road Highgate in 1905, and the upstairs lending library, with 20,000 volumes, when opened the following year, was named in honour of Robert Spears (Islington Library Services Information Leaflet, 1996).

His work did not stop there, and at the age of 70, in addition to his Highgate ministry, editing the *Christian Life,* and contributing regularly to other popular journals like the *Unitarian Bible Magazine,* 'he had for some years past the whole or partial oversight of our cause at Walthamstow, Southend, Newcastle-under-Lyne and Longton, Barnard Castle, King's Lynn, Bury St Edmunds and Deal. In reviving dying causes or initiating new ones he had no equal' (*CL,* 4 March 1899). Spears' day-to-day support for other Unitarian causes like the Central Postal Mission, which sent out material to enquirers, is too great to describe in detail. He died after a short illness, still active until within a few weeks of his death in the midst of his large (and apparently happy) family. His gravestone still stands in Nunhead Cemetery. He married first **Margaret Kirton** (1818–1867) in 1846, with whom he had five children, of whom only the youngest survived him; and secondly in 1869 **Emily Glover** (1835–1917), with whom he had six children.

An evaluation

Robert Spears was seen by all as a man of action. 'Do it now' was his motto, otherwise he would never have the time. 'He never delegated anything, but found a fresh task for every helper' (*CL*, 25 March 1899). Holidays did not interest him, although on at least two visits abroad in the 1880s he expanded the range of his contacts. All, however, was subordinated to the expansion of Unitarianism, or more correctly the variety of it that he espoused. Of course he had his critics, and his essentially non-intellectual steam-roller approach did not suit everyone. *Courtney S. Kenny, writing an appreciation in the *The Christian Life* to which he had been a very regular contributor, observed that 'some have thought of him as a doctrinaire who imposed on others his own dogmas, and limited the range of co-operation by the range of his own convictions' – although Kenny himself did not find it so (*CL*, 4 March 1899). *The Universalist Leader* in the USA probably got him just about right:

> He was a large-hearted generous companionable man; fairly ablaze
> with enthusiasm on behalf of Unitarianism of the Channing
> type, while impatient at the inroads of extreme opinions which
> undermine the authority of the Scriptures and of Jesus Christ as
> the spiritual leader of mankind. He saw no use for any form of
> Unitarianism that was not founded on a distinctively Christian basis.
> (*CL*, 22 April 1899)

As might be expected, the appreciations of him in *The Inquirer* at the time of his death were less fulsome:

> Mr Spears has not seldom lamented the narrow limit of his
> education and the provincialism which clung to him throughout his
> life. Himself a man of restless energy he was apt to disregard the
> slow and careful methods by which business is usually safeguarded.
> The large body of work he accomplished was done in spite of
> difficulties and it is certain that those who knew him best were
> most attracted towards him. He was a warm hearted and generous

helper, and was as ready to do a good turn for a distressed opponent as for one of his own party.

(*Inq* 25 March 1899)

Robert Spears charmed and influenced men and women from all walks of life, notably wealthy Unitarians who shared his viewpoint and subsidised his many activities. His message and the force of his personality (given greater prophetic emphasis by his full beard) created several congregations and enhanced others, some of which still exist. The last word should come from Spears on himself, in a text which sums up his vision:

Forty years ago I entered on my duties with a sense that I was called to work of this kind, and yet I had no special aptitudes, had no college or ministerial training, no family prestige, and had the disadvantage of a northern dialect or brogue ... if I had life to live over again, it would be done with the old name, 'a Unitarian minister'; and nothing I know of would win me from that straight line of duty. I have not simply founded or recovered to life a dozen churches, and established nine Sunday-schools and three journals, and helped into existence other useful institutions, but I could tell how, with the help of God, I have been the means of sorrows lessened, of joys heightened, of lives made more bright and pure, of hearts made more strong, homes made happier, and of gratitude expressed a thousand times for our gospel of Unitarianism. I do not deny that other ministers, and Unitarian churches, have done more good work; but I do protest against the idea that the Unitarian name stands in the way of religious and social usefulness.

(*CL*, 31 October 1891)

Sources

Christian Life 5 August 1876; 31 October 1891; 4, 11 and 25 March 1899.

Inquirer 21 February 1874; 11, 18 and 25 March 1876.

Thomas, R., 1969, *TUHS*.

UUCA (Ulster Unitarian Christian Association), 1903, *Memorials of Robert Spears.*

Webb, R. K., in *Oxford DNB*.

Spears family tree supplied by Dr John R Spears, now at Dr Williams's Library.

From *Transactions of the Unitarian Historical Society*, 1999

11 The Unitarian Field Marshal

The papers of **Rev. J Arthur Pearson** 1870–1947 (for their location, see
TUHS 1993) show that in 1898, during his first ministry at Oldham, he
became the founding editor of a short-lived Unitarian monthly called *The
New Kingdom*. It was not successful in attracting the necessary readership
and it closed in 1900. Among the items that Arthur Pearson retained from
his brief editorship were letters from well-known Unitarians to whom he
had written. This is a response that he received in 1898 to his request for
an article:

Lordswood Southampton 31 January 1898

*I regret I cannot meet your wish to write an article for the Unitarian
journal named 'The New Kingdom'. It is not that I have changed my
views as to the unity of the God head – far from it – for the longer I live the
more do I hold that the life and works of Jesus Christ as given in the New
Testament afford no sanction for the doctrine of a trinity...*

Yours truly
Neville Chamberlain

Was this letter from the man who later became the Prime Minister? While
brought up in the Unitarian faith, and retaining a nominal connection
with it, Neville Chamberlain the politician was known in later life for his
coyness on religious matters, uneasy when attending religious services of
any description. A letter from the then young businessman, just returned
to England from living abroad, would be a notable find. However, when I
examined it something appeared to be wrong: the handwriting was that
of an older man, on black-edged notepaper, and Southampton was not a
location associated with the Chamberlain family. Therefore I contacted
Professor David Dilks, Vice Chancellor of the University of Hull, who had
written a biography of the Prime Minister. He responded immediately:
'Perhaps it is from the pen of the distinguished soldier of that name?'

Further researches proved that this was the case, and they revealed a fascinating story. The life of ***Field Marshal Sir Neville Bowles Chamberlain** (1820–1902) is recorded in most biographical dictionaries covering this period. He was one of the leaders of British India from the 1850s to the 1870s. With almost foolhardy personal bravery it was Chamberlain who did much to re-impose British rule around Delhi after the Indian Mutiny of 1857.

He signed up with the East India Co as an ensign at the age of 18, and by the age of 28 he had served in three campaigns – Afgan, Gwalior and the Punjab – and had been wounded at least ten times. In the Indian Mutiny he took a leading part in driving back the mutineers in Delhi. 'Seeing the men hesitate before an enclosure wall lined with the enemy, he set them an example by leading his horse over it, but got a ball in his shoulder' (*The Times*, February 1902). The culmination of his career was his command of the newly raised Punjab irregular force. 'That force probably saved India in 1857 ... Sir Neville though a gladiator par excellence and a blood stained warrior... was ever loath to draw the sword except as a last resort' (*The Times*, March 1902).

Honours followed, and a developing political ability meant that he became a general in 1875, with the command of the Madras army in the following year. He retired in 1881 to Lordswood, near Southampton, and a life of comparative solitude. With his eldest brother an admiral and two other brothers generals, it seems out of character for Sir Neville to have become a Unitarian and a member of the Liberal Party with fairly advanced views. In the army he had clearly been a strict disciplinarian, but he was rather different in private life.

The Unitarian

There is no doubt of the strength of his Unitarian convictions, although his faith is mentioned in few biographical articles. He began to attend the Southampton church during the ministry of **Rev. Iden Payne** (1874–76), presumably in 1874, because soon after that he had to return to India (E. J. Spencer, *Southern Unitarian Association Chronicle*, January 1937). There is a full obituary in *The Inquirer*, 22 February 1902, written by **Rev. Shaen**

Solly, who was the minister at the Church of the Saviour, Southampton, from 1882 to 1888:

> After his retirement Sir Neville lived at Lordswood. He joined our
> Church, and became a liberal subscriber to its funds, though during
> the lifetime of his wife (she died in 1896), who was a Churchwoman,
> he generally attended service with her. After her death he felt at
> liberty to come regularly to our Unitarian worship, and he was
> generous in his donations. Quite recently he gave £1000 to the
> British & Foreign Unitarian Association. His simple-hearted modesty
> and intense dislike of anything in the nature of parade prevented
> his ever coming forward as a personal leader of our cause ...We may
> indeed be proud of having such a man in our household of faith.

To the B&FUA he had donated £1000 for its own funds, plus another £1000 which was made into a separate trust, known as the Chamberlain Fund, for the benefit of the Unitarian church in Southampton.

According to Emily Bushrod, who provided references for this article, it was understood that Sir Neville disliked being asked whether he had a family connection with the famous Birmingham Chamberlains, who were also Unitarian in background; there was no family connection, although it is likely that he and Joseph Chamberlain would have met at some stage.

The funeral

His funeral at Rownhams, conducted by the Vicar, was a complex affair, at the wish of the War Office rather than that of Sir Neville. *The Times* account records a big military component with a gun carriage, a 17-gun salute, and (together with the many generals present) a personal representative of the Kaiser. The local newspapers reveal a striking difference in their reports of Sir Neville's Unitarian associations. *The Hampshire Advertiser, The Hampshire Independent,* and *The Southampton Observer and News,* all of 22 February 1902, merely reported that E. C. Bennett attended the funeral ceremony (**Rev. E. C. Bennett** was then the Unitarian minister at Southampton).

These newspapers had a mainly Anglican readership, but the *Southampton News and Hampshire Express* regularly covered nonconformist events. On the same day it reported that a pew at the funeral was reserved for the Unitarian minister and three representatives of the Church, plus another from the B&FUA. It announced that a memorial service would be held at the Unitarian church the following day. The newspaper added:

> Sir Neville considered the Concentration Camps in South Africa a terrible mistake ... he frankly said (of the war mongers) that it was hopeless work trying to convert the aristocracy and the Church of England to Liberal and peaceful principles ... In religion he had been for many years a convinced and devoted Unitarian ... His piety was simple and sincere. He defended his absence from the Established Church on the grounds that 'he could not worship according to the Anglican faith and then to God in another. ... He preferred frankness in this matter as in all others.'

A correspondent in a later issue (8 March) concluded: 'His Unitarian Christianity made him more Christian than the multitude of Christians (so called) who, like their Government, thirst for Dutch blood.'

Sir Neville was clearly a complicated and contradictory character of a kind which seemed to abound in Victorian England. He was an authoritarian who on retirement decided to take a very different stand. He was created a Field Marshal at the age of 80, an honour in old age. Surely this is the only example of such an appointment, honouring someone who was at the time a member of, and a regular attender at, a Unitarian Church.

Note: Various reference works on sport state that Colonel Sir Neville Chamberlain invented the game of snooker in Southern India for officers under his command, as an adaptation of billiards. This was not Sir Neville Bowles Chamberlain but his nephew Sir Neville Francis Fitzgerald Chamberlain (1856–1944), who had no Unitarian connections. See the Oxford Dictionary of National Biography.

From *Transactions of the Unitarian Historical Society*, 1993

12 Unitarian Trust Funds: the Hibbert and the Rawdon

Rev. G. Stephen Spinks, writing about trust funds, observed that 'the history of charitable trusts tends of necessity to become a list of names, dates and monies expended, the real content of the record and the widespread nature of the resultant good being lost under the respectability of procedure and legal requirement' (*Hibbert Journal*, July 1952).

It is often true that the lists to which Spinks refers are made the central theme of their work, although this is to take a limited view of charitable religious trusts. The background to their formation and the interaction of the trustees make a far more revealing and interesting story and are no less important in enabling an assessment of their long-term operation. The reasons for the creation of trusts generally reflect a perceived long-term need, and the trust deed often marks the final resolution of different, competing and clashing views. Sometimes what went on before their formation can be of greater significance than their subsequent work, although in other instances the reverse is true. This article compares the origins and early histories of the Hibbert and Rawdon trust funds, and shows that their activities reflected different interpretations of Unitarianism in the first half of the nineteenth century. They were formed at about the same time, in the 1850s, and were closely associated with organised Unitarianism. By the 1870s each had pursued its own path, guided largely by the attitude of the early trustees to the meaning of the vague wording of the original deed.

The story begins in 1813 with the passing of what is known as the Trinity Act, which legalised the holding of Unitarian beliefs, and was seen by many to be the vital step towards full religious liberty. The Act created optimism and great hopes for the future. As E. M. Wilbur says in his *A History of Unitarianism* (1952, p. 345), 'timidity had given way to bold aggressiveness'. This was expressed in organisational form in 1819 by the formation of the 'Unitarian Association for Protecting the Civil Rights of Unitarians', which merged with other similar societies in May 1825 to form the British and Foreign Unitarian Association, whose foundation can be said to mark the start of Unitarian denominationalism.

In its early years the B&FUA was notably unsuccessful, in that by 1827 there were only 34 congregations affiliated to it out of a possible 200. The figure never rose above 80, and for most of its early life it was just an association of individuals rather than an association of churches. Many believed, as others have done since, that such an association with a theological title would limit the freedom and independence of congregations. Many of the congregations were English Presbyterian in origin and they wished to stand alone, free from external constraints, with no wish to apply the Unitarian name to their meeting houses or chapels.

To complicate matters, a new group had come on to the scene who wanted to make the title 'Presbyterian' solely their own. Scottish ministers often migrated with their congregations into England as the demand for labour created by new industry increased. They brought with them their own widely accepted version of Presbyterianism, wrapped up generally in a modified Calvinism, and after forming the Presbyterian Church of England in 1836 they sought to deny the old Presbyterians/Unitarians their title. This led grant-aiding bodies like the Widows Fund of Lancashire and Cheshire to move towards the use of the Unitarian name, in order not to be forced to include the Scottish Calvinists within the scope of their Fund.

The legal decisions arising out of the Lady Hewley case, with the courts finding that chapels and trusts founded before the Trinity Act 1813 was passed could not be termed Unitarian, had an impact on the old English Presbyterian congregations whose members' beliefs were Unitarian. All this had an unnerving effect, and for over a decade from 1833 until 1844, when the Dissenters' Chapels Bill was passed, the Unitarian movement stagnated. As Fred Kenworthy wrote in *The Inquirer* (6 June 1959), 'the fear that the old meeting houses and funds would be lost had an effect that was depressing in the extreme. Buildings were neglected and congregations dispirited, gradually growing smaller: in the country districts a considerable number of them became extinct.'

Therefore when the Dissenters' Chapels Bill became an Act, most Unitarians breathed a sigh of relief. Many of the old chapels could hardly be called active in 1850, and in Kenworthy's view that year marked the lowest point in the period of depression. Thereafter and into the 1870s, British Unitarianism showed real signs of revival and expansion. Between 1850 and 1875 more than sixty chapels were rebuilt or entirely renovated, while 31 congregations were founded in the same period, i.e. at the rate of more than one a year.

Unitarianism in 1850

The disputes and uncertainties that had arisen since 1813 had left their mark. These scarring experiences precluded an even greater expansion of the movement after 1850. Fred Kenworthy (op. cit.) sums up the effect:

> Certainly the Dissenters' Chapels Act removed a paralysing fear, that the ancient Meeting houses which had become Unitarian would be lost to the movement. On the other hand, the struggle for the Act had discouraged doctrinal propaganda; men were afraid of clear and definite teaching lest it should become dogmatic and imperil the principle of freedom on which the claim to possession of the old meeting houses had mainly rested.

> One result of this attitude may be noted in a report of Rev. Hugh Hutton to the British and Foreign Unitarian Association. In 1852 he was appointed their Home Agent and Missionary (as he was called); he held the office for four years, during which he visited many parts of the country. He described one bar to progress as 'the avowed disinclination of a large number of the better educated and more wealthy members of our Churches to give any part of their sympathy or support to efforts aiming at the diffusion of a knowledge of our religious principles in a doctrinal form or under the Unitarian name; this difficulty has met me in various forms during the whole progress of my missionary work.' So the effect of the Act was only partly liberating; some still felt averse to zeal and enthusiasm or clear doctrinal teaching. But where others were missionary-minded, the Act had removed any forbidding bar to progress.

These two tendencies – one to take a non-doctrinal unsectarian approach, the other to proclaim Unitarianism as the faith of the future – affected the whole movement.

While all the litigation was in progress, nobody was going to create a new trust fund for the benefit of Unitarianism, for fear that it might be brought before the courts and be alienated from its original purposes. The 1844 Act released the stopper: thereafter it was safe to create funds associated with Unitarianism. It is thus no coincidence that in the 1850s several Unitarian benevolent funds were created, one example being the Ministers' Benevolent Fund in 1852. However, our concern here is with the two most important funds formed in this period: the Hibbert Trust and the Rawdon Fund, the latter now known as The Ministers' Stipend Augmentation Fund.

They began almost in the same way, and they were based on very similar principles, but by the 1870s they looked different ways: one following a non-sectarian approach, the other a specifically Unitarian line. They became, in short, two strands of the denominational history, reflecting what had happened in the previous half-century.

Robert Hibbert

First, the Hibbert Trust. *Robert Hibbert, a former owner of slaves in the West Indies, is a shadowy figure, but he was without doubt a strong assertive Unitarian. Details of his life are scarce, and no portrait of him exists. Born in 1770, he married in the 1790s but died childless in 1849. He left a will which created a fund, to be called the Anti-Trinitarian Fund, to be set up after his wife's death, which occurred in 1853. Hibbert's aim was undoubtedly that the Fund should help learned Unitarian divines to mount attacks against the doctrine of the Trinity, which he hoped would assist in the final nemesis of the Church of England, of which he had a considerable dislike.

Hibbert was advised by *Edwin Wilkins Field (1804–71), a leading solicitor and one of the most influential Unitarian laymen in the period 1830 to 1850. A man of great energy and wide-ranging interests, he was the son of the Presbyterian-cum-Unitarian minister at Warwick and exemplified the English Presbyterian tradition. It was he who organised the Unitarian lobby that helped to secure the passing of the 1844 Act. He argued against using the word 'Unitarian' in the scheme that set up Hibbert's fund, as 'our Law Courts would be sure to fix some improper meaning on it' (*Hibbert Journal* 1953), as well as insisting on the condition that Hibbert's trustees could not be taken before the courts as a result of any of their decisions.

Hibbert took Field's advice on both these points and made the trust sufficiently wide and open that its objectives could be interpreted by trustees in accordance with changing times. He was, however, very clear on one point: all recipients of his money must be heterodox in their religious beliefs, and above all must be committed to the 'spread of Christianity in its simplest and most intelligible form', a phrase which Robert Hibbert believed to be synonymous with Unitarianism. He wanted his Fund to be for the benefit of the best products of the training colleges for the Unitarian ministry, and on no account must any money be applied to church buildings.

The first 18 trustees were appointed in 1853, consisting of leading and wealthy Unitarian laymen. Most were from the south of England, but there were also cotton manufacturers from Manchester. Ministers could not be appointed to serve as Hibbert Trustees. The trustees wrote to prominent Unitarian ministers, asking for their written suggestions as to how the open schedule should be interpreted. The result of this activity was the creation of a scheme of scholarships, based on stringent and competitive written examinations for the students of Manchester New College, newly located at University Hall in Gordon Square, London (now occupied by Dr Williams's Library).

These negotiations were conducted in relative secrecy, and all that the Unitarian public knew of the Fund was contained in a public announcement, followed by an article written by Field in the *Christian Reformer* in April 1853. The battle lines were drawn even at this stage, as the *Christian Reformer* represented the assertive Unitarian line. Field was clearly of the other school and wrote in the article: 'I dare say that many or most of your readers will, more or less, differ from my views as to the decline of the influence of our ministers, and of our modes of thought on the general public'. The editor, **R. Brook Aspland**, could not resist a final dig: 'We desire our readers to observe that while we gladly insert Mr. Field's letter, we do not profess to adopt all his opinions.' A clash of views was bound to take place.

Christopher Rawdon and his trust fund

It is now necessary to consider the foundation and early history of the Rawdon Fund. ***Christopher Rawdon** (1780–1858) was a Lancashire mill-owner and merchant, and a staunch Unitarian, like his father before him, though at Todmorden in Yorkshire. He and his brother James, who died in 1855, were wealthy, and after the 1830s their names can be seen at or near the top of most subscription lists associated with the Unitarian cause, especially in Liverpool, where they lived. Christopher's name and armorial shield are set in stained glass in a window of the main hall of Dr Williams's Library in Gordon Square in London. Christopher Rawdon had a wider education than many Unitarians, in that he was educated as a child in Switzerland and was fluent in Portuguese. How he learned this language is an arresting tale:

> In the early 1790s business took his father from time to time
> to Portugal, and on one occasion, while waiting wind-bound at
> Falmouth, he met there a Portuguese gentleman who had just
> arrived from Lisbon. During their time together they discussed
> the advantages of giving children in very early life a knowledge
> of foreign languages, and Mr. Rawdon mentioned the common
> custom in Switzerland for parents in the French and German
> cantons to exchange children for a time with this in view. The
> idea so pleased Senor de Paiva that he immediately proposed to
> Mr. Rawdon to send his son Christopher to Lisbon, and to take in
> exchange his nephew. After some hesitation, Mr. Rawdon consented
> to this sudden proposal, and, before Senor de Paiva left, he wrote
> the following order, which a few weeks afterwards that gentleman
> presented in person:

Dear Wife — Deliver to the bearer thy first-born.
Signed: Christopher Rawdon

Whatever may have been the feelings of the mother on this first intimation to her of the arrangement made at Falmouth, she knew too well the decision of her husband's character to hesitate a moment in yielding obedience. A servant was forthwith despatched to Otley, where young Christopher was spending his holidays with his grandfather, and on his arrival he was handed over to Senor de Paiva, who carried him to Lisbon and kept him as one of his own children for upwards of a year.

(Obituary, *Christian Reformer* 1858)

Christopher Rawdon was also a businessman of firm and distinct views, and he saw the Lady Hewley case as 'a direct branch from the bitter root of religious intolerance, as embodied in Creeds and Establishments, and it became one of the cravings of his heart, a thing absolutely necessary to his peace, that he should do something to repair the injustice committed, and stop the mischief that might ensue' (*Christian Reformer* 1858). Like Robert Hibbert, he was strongly opposed to the Church of England, and it is clear that a major motivation of the founders of two of the largest trust funds associated with Unitarianism today was a detestation of the Anglican Church. It appears that the public announcement of the formation of Hibbert's Trust provided the initial impetus for the Rawdon Fund's creation.

By the time of Field's letter in the *Christian Reformer*, Rawdon had begun contacting wealthy Unitarians, mainly in the North, to gather together £20,000 for a fund to benefit ministers' stipends. In writing for a donation on 15th April 1853 to one of these, he enclosed a copy of the Hibbert Deed, stating: 'I venture the opinion that you will consider the Hibbert bequest as affecting in no small degree the scheme which I and my brother have so much at heart, and as a not unfitting sequel to so noble an example.' The sentence which followed could equally have been written by Robert Hibbert: 'Does all this not show the present to be a favourable moment for joining in one grand effort in the endeavour to stem the rapidly swelling tide of sacerdotal assumption of dominion over the whole civilised world?' Thus the aim of both founders was not to sustain or defend the existing position, but to provide a means of better attacking orthodox Christianity, leading eventually to the triumph of Unitarian Christianity.

The £20,000 was finally obtained, the Rawdons providing £4,000, and the Deed of the Ministers' Stipend Augmentation Fund was executed in 1856. Aimed at raising stipends, it was designed to meet those areas of need not covered by the Hibbert Trust. The Deed is very similar to Hibbert's scheme and, like that document, did not mention Unitarianism. Its object was 'to encourage the faithful Ministers of congregations in England assembled for the public worship of God, the Members, Communicants or Ministers whereof shall not be required to subscribe or assent to any Articles of religious belief, or to submit to any test of religious doctrine'. Preference was to be given to ministers who had attended a training college, and no grants were to run beyond a single year without re-application. It was stated that 'Congregations situated north of the River Trent shall claim the first consideration of the Committee'.

The trust funds in operation

By 1860 both funds were in operation and setting precedents in the entirely new area of allocating grants. Neither was in danger of being challenged before the Courts. Both were certainly benefiting Unitarianism in one way or another and assisting in its expansion. However, they were doing little to bring about the downfall of the Established Church. As both funds had independent trustees, with deeds which did not limit them, the trustees developed each fund to meet their own tastes, based on broad principles set out in the original deed. The object of the Hibbert Trust was to assist 'Christianity in its simplest and most intelligible form'; and the object of the Rawdon Fund was to help ministers of congregations with no religious tests except the acknowledgement that the 'Old and New Testaments contain a record of Divine Revelation'. Both these simple definitions were the founders' code words for Unitarianism. Apart from these remits, the trustees had a free hand to operate as they wished.

In 1874 *Jerom Murch (1807–1895) produced his privately printed *Memoir of the life of Robert Hibbert, and the history of the Hibbert Trust to date.* Intended to inform enquirers and new trustees who had not known Hibbert, it was favourably reviewed in *The Inquirer* on 25 July 1874. But *The Inquirer* later turned to the attack, and a long editorial on 5 September shot the first bullets in what proved to be a long and angry exchange between strong personalities with firm views. Admitting that in 21 years several well-known students had won valuable scholarships in honourable competition, **Rev. T. L. Marshall** (1825–1915), the editor, asked what benefit had accrued to 'those who have devoted their lives to faithful and efficient ministerial duty on the most inadequate stipends'. In his view this was contrary to the wishes of the founder, and he put the points even more strongly when donning his editorial hat:

> But a portion of the public which this journal professes to represent
> seems at a loss to know what special advantage has resulted to
> our churches, or what contributions have been made to the noble
> literature of a Free Theology, which would not have been given to
> the world had the Trust never existed.

What had really annoyed Marshall was the Hibbert Trust's introduction in 1873 of travelling scholarships of £200 a year for graduates of any British university. Conditional only on a simple declaration on the lines of Hibbert's will, the scholarships were not designed specifically for people wishing to become ministers of religion. Of the 69 applicants, none of the four appointed had any connection with Unitarianism. Marshall fumed: 'One at least of the successful candidates is well known at Oxford as an extreme High Churchman'. The simple declaration was not enough: candidates could believe anything.

The battle was on, with the attack coming from the anti-Martineau section of Unitarianism, who believed that the Hibbert Trust was just a cabal to foster Martineau's advocacy of Free Christianity, rather than

Unitarianism specifically. Thus the Trust became the subject of strife, and the subsequent argument was bad tempered.

In succeeding months, thousands of words on the issue appeared in *The Inquirer*. Those who had known Hibbert wrote in to say what they recalled his views to be; virtually all pointed out that he was a devoted Unitarian who wished specifically to benefit its ministry. Murch and other trustees had their views printed in *The Inquirer*, but Marshall kept up the attack (12 September 1874):

> It appears to be an unquestionable fact that our bitterest theological opponents will henceforth almost exclusively benefit by a scheme quite alien to the original objects of the Trust, carried out by Trustees elected on account of their presumed sympathy with the distinctively Unitarian sentiments of the Founder, and every one of whom is known to be more or less connected with the Unitarian denomination. And we are expected to admire this as unsectarian liberality!

James Taplin, minister at Kingswood, Birmingham, was perhaps a little more temperate, though no less forthright (*Inq*,19 September 1874):

> I believe the Trustees, however sincere in their intention, have seriously departed from the wishes of the Testator ... and could he rise from his grave, he would lift up his voice in condemnation of all the acts tending to encourage the growth of orthodox errors and impede the sacred interests of Christian truth and freedom.

But it is the unsigned pieces that are really sharp. For example, an anonymous writer in the issue of 3 October 1874 concluded: 'we may at least compliment the Trustees on the remarkable ingenuity they have shown in dispensing with almost every condition which the benevolent founder regarded as essential to his scheme ... it is time to say publicly that the Trustees should hand over the Trust to those who can administer it more in accordance with the known wishes of the Founder.' In the issue of 5 December 1874, the trustees were asked when they were going to advertise and open their meetings to the public, as required in the schedule to the deed, and the arrangement was challenged by which they dined together at the expense of the Trust — 'which is almost the only clause that the Trustees have rigidly adhered to'. Almost the last exchange in the debate, this article called upon the trustees to resign, as 'we have adduced enough evidence to show that we are acquainted with no Trust in modern times which has been more completely perverted from the objects contemplated by the Founder'.

Throughout the debate, correspondents were making comparisons with the Rawdon Fund, whose trustees were judged to be highly virtuous. The two funds were about the same size at this time, with a capital of about £25,000 each. Taplin wrote in *The Inquirer* on 26 September 1874: 'Evidence has for years been given, testifying to the value of the Ministers' Stipend Augmentation Fund. Not only is it a valuable boon in sustaining and promoting Liberal Christianity, but it has stimulated one congregation at least to do more for its minister than it ever did before, rather than receive extraneous aid. This Fund, which has now been conducted with the highest advantage for years past, is confined to a certain locality, and may be regarded as a good model for the future action of the Hibbert Trustees, who in adopting it may extend the good.'

By 1875 the debate had petered out, and the Hibbert Trustees made it quite clear that they were going to ignore the whole matter, as no action could be taken against them in the courts. They did not even mention the dispute in the minutes of their meetings.

Taking different paths

The Rawdon Fund and the Hibbert Trust started out with similar basic tools: an open deed, £20,000 in capital, and wealthy Unitarian laymen as trustees. By 1874 the Rawdon Trustees had taken their non-doctrinaire remit and turned their Fund, by the use of precedent, into one that could benefit Unitarian stipends only. There were many reasons for this turn of events, but undoubtedly one of the chief was the focus of the Fund on the north of England, and Lancashire and Yorkshire in particular. This area of the country was influenced by that strand of missionary, assertive Unitarianism that arose after 1813, based on the work of people like **Robert Aspland** and ***Richard Wright**, a Unitarian missionary who travelled the country.

The trustees of Christopher Rawdon created a Unitarian Fund such as the founder undoubtedly wanted; they were all from the north of England and followed the kind of Unitarianism that they encountered in their chapels. Thus in the opinion of the correspondents in *The Inquirer* who wanted Unitarian congregations and ministers to benefit, the Rawdon Trustees were judged to be acting rightly. While the trustees supported traditional Unitarianism, nobody would challenge the Fund's operation, and so it has proved to this day. The Ministers' Stipend Augmentation Fund has consistently fulfilled its task with quiet efficiency, to the undoubted benefit of Unitarian ministers and congregations.

In comparison, what happened to the Hibbert Trust? Some of the early Hibbert Trustees came from Manchester, but in the 1860s there was a bitter argument over the payment of travelling expenses, as the trust mainly met in London. The Trust decided, after obtaining Counsel's opinion, that such expenses were not to be paid, so most of the trustees from the northern England withdrew, leaving the majority living in the locality of London. Many of these remaining trustees had English Presbyterian origins and followed the non-sectarian approach. James Martineau's ideas undoubtedly exercised an influence over the Trust which led it away from a specifically Unitarian line, as Hibbert's open deed allowed. In the debates of the 1870s they seemed to do everything they could which would upset the traditional Bible-based Unitarians.

We may well ask: did the Hibbert Trustees fulfil the wishes of their founder? Undoubtedly he intended to allow them wide discretion, but Robert Hibbert appears to have been a rather narrow-minded Unitarian, and without the influence of E. W. Field he would have prepared his trust deed in a very different way. The open nature of the deed and the personalities of the first trustees could only mean that with the passage of time support would be given to those who were not heterodox Unitarians; this would not have met with Hibbert's approval. In this sense, the Hibbert Trustees were not following the known wishes and desires of their founder. However, this raises what has proved to be a perennial issue. Hibbert wanted his trust to support 'the spread of Christianity in its most simple and intelligible form'. To him this phrase could mean nothing else but Unitarianism, which is why it satisfied him. But, as Field very clearly saw as early as the 1840s, the connection between the two might not always be the same. *C. J. Montefiore, writing on this issue from a non-Unitarian position, pointed out a few problems:

> Are the words a mere synonym for Unitarianism? Is it necessarily
> the case that, in religion, what is simplest is truest? May not truth
> be many-sided and even complex? If that be so, it would seem not
> improbable that Christianity 'in its most simple and intelligible
> form' need not necessarily be the truest kind of Christianity. When
> we speak of Christianity in its 'most intelligible form' we are
> inclined to ask: most intelligible to whom? To the man in the street?
> But is he the best judge? Perhaps the most 'intelligible' form of
> Christianity to a philosopher would be exceedingly unintelligible to
> the man in the street. But these problems must be left unanswered.

(Book review, *Hibbert Journal*, July 1933)

The name of Hibbert has become widely known, largely owing to the broad interpretation of the trust deed adopted by the trustees. Ventures like the Hibbert Lectures, the Hibbert Journal, and Hibbert Houses would probably have been impossible if the founder's intentions had been strictly met. Perhaps St. Paul's words (II Corinthians, chapter 3) apply to trust funds of any kind as much as to anything else:

> Our sufficiency is from God, who has qualified us to be ministers
> of a new covenant, not in a written code but in the Spirit; for the
> written code kills, but the Spirit gives life.

Sources

Christian Reformer 1856, 1858.

Davie, D., 1982, *Dissentient Voice*, University of Notre Dame Press, USA.

Lee, S. G., 1953, *Hibbert Journal*.

McLachlan, H., 1937, *The Widows Fund Association*, privately printed.

Oxford Dictionary of National Biography.

Wilbur, E. M., 1952, *A History of Unitarianism*, Harvard University Press.

Wilson, H. G., 1951, 'Ministers' Benevolent Fund', *TUHS*.

From *Transactions of the Unitarian Historical Society, 1985,*
based on the Presidential Address given to the Unitarian Historical Society
at Manchester College Oxford, April 1983

The
Twentieth
Century

13 Killed fighting for their country: two Unitarian ministers

The First World War swept away nineteenth century England for good, and with it went nineteenth century Nonconformity. For those with eyes to see, the slowing down of Nonconformist expansion had been apparent long before. But the war produced a new crisis of faith, and dissolved many traditional values.

These words, written by David M. Thompson in 1972 in his collection of readings entitled *Nonconformity in the 19th Century* (p. 229), reflect the now universally received view of the enormous social impact of the War. While the part played by the various churches in World War I has been described in numerous books, there is nothing, as far as I know, on the role specifically played by Unitarians in the War, their attitudes towards it, and its effect on them. It is only in recent times that researchers have started to look at the history of British Unitarianism post-1914.

It would be valuable to test the proposition that there was a significant shift in outlook between 1914 and 1918, and that optimism drained away from the Unitarian movement during these years: a trend from which it never recovered. Before the War, 'the Five Precepts' – created by **Rev. James Freeman Clarke** in the Middle West of the USA in the nineteenth century – had held great sway within Unitarianism in Britain, affirming *The Fatherhood of God, The Brotherhood of Man, The Leadership of Jesus, Salvation by Character, and The Progress of Mankind, onwards and upwards for ever;* but the last two precepts virtually disappeared from view after the War, as the positive outlook that they represented could no longer be sustained. In 1914 British Unitarianism had possibly 40,000 adherents, and the relatively large numbers involved in the hostilities certainly suggest that the horrors of the War touched many; by 1918 it was estimated that 7,000 Unitarians had served in the forces, and that about 1,000 people connected with Unitarian churches had been killed (*Inq* 4 November 1916; 26 January 1918).

This article is an attempt to direct the attention of historians towards an examination of Unitarian attitudes to 'the War to end Wars', and its impact in Britain. My contention is that the decline of Unitarian strength in Britain dates back into the nineteenth century, and that World War I accelerated rather than initiated the process. Therefore I would agree with Dr Thompson's conclusion, adding that in the case of Unitarianism the onset of the decline can be traced back to factors that arose before 1880.

I want to open the debate by examining the lives and attitudes of the only two Unitarian ministers killed on active service during the War: **Edward Stanley Russell** and **Walter Short**. Both began in the ranks but became commissioned officers (Captains) and served in front-line regiments, though in different theatres of war: Russell in the Near East, and Short in France. One was educated at Oxford, the other at Manchester, and both had university degrees. There were no Unitarian chaplains appointed during the War. However, **Rev. T. P. Spedding** was recognised by the War Office as its pastoral visitor to Unitarians in the forces in the UK, working on behalf of the British and Foreign Unitarian Association.

Unitarian ministers were exempt from conscription, but both Russell and Short enlisted well before the Conscription Act came into force in 1916. This Act, which exempted all recognised ministers of religion from conscription, did not deter several ministers from joining in the war effort by volunteering to serve in the Royal Army Medical Corps, the Ambulance Service, or the Young Men's Christian Association, often at advanced ages. Perhaps the most well-known example was **Rev. Mortimer Rowe**, who was awarded the Military Medal for his devoted work at the Western Front, returning home in 1918 suffering from gas poisoning; he wrote very regularly and at length for *The Inquirer* under the undramatic heading 'Field Ambulance Notes'. It was this column that brought Rowe to the attention of the Unitarian public and helped him on his way to become the first General Secretary of the General Assembly in 1929.

Rowe and Russell were fellow students at Manchester College Oxford (MCO). I turn first to the complex and enigmatic character of Edward Russell.

Edward Stanley Russell

E. S. Russell was born at Weston-Super-Mare on 11 June 1882, the fifth child of a family of six, and the youngest of four sons. His father was Rev. John Roebuck Russell, a Baptist minister then in charge of the church in Bristol Road, who remained active among the Baptists into the 1920s.

Baptist origins

The young Russell was surrounded by religion, as his mother Emilee was related to a number of Baptist ministers. The family lived on the North Lancashire coast from the time when he was two until he was six, when they moved to High Wycombe, where most of his boyhood was spent.

We owe our extensive knowledge of Russell to the determination of **Rev. Arnold Heynes Lewis** (1878–1968), who in 1918 wrote a biography of his fellow student and close friend. Assembled with the aid of letters from relatives and friends, this glowing eulogy not surprisingly failed to find a publisher. The manuscript and certain of the letters went to Lewis' younger son John, who passed the items to me in 1992. They are now lodged at Harris Manchester College and the Imperial War Museum (war material only).

As a teenager, there was not even the slightest suggestion from Russell of a likely move away from the Baptists. He seems to have had little schooling of note, and a commercial life was seen as the best course, given his ready tongue and engaging personality. He spent a period as a successful commercial salesman of ink in Glasgow. He was fully involved in churches wherever he went, and was a natural magnet for young people. In 1903 he took the obvious course and entered Regent's Park College, then in London, to train for the Baptist ministry, registering the following year at University College to read for an Arts degree. It was at Regent's Park that he met Lewis, who had been there since 1899 and who had, if anything, more Baptist ministers in his family than did Russell. What happened next is best described in Lewis's words:

> *Russell had scarcely begun his second year at College, when he began to entertain misgivings as to his fitness for the Baptist ministry. His*

convictions were deepening, his ardour for the work increasing: but he found himself less and less able to cast his beliefs into the phraseology and formulae to which the churches were accustomed. In particular he inclined to a pantheistic view of God. and was more disposed to assert the general divinity of human life than the unique Deity of Christ.

He left in 1905, 'to the great regret of the Committee and the Tutor', but continued with studies for his degree, which he took in 1907. Believing that the ministry was the future for him, he looked around for a theological college which he could with conscience join as a preface to entering the ministry of an as-yet-unspecified denomination. He applied to become a student at MCO on the suggestion of one of his former tutors, Dr W. R. Boyce Gibson. This would lead in the natural course of events to ministry among the Unitarians, though there is little evidence that he knew much about them, apart from talks that he had with another University tutor in London, **Rev. Dr. G. Dawes Hicks**, then also the Unitarian minister at Islington.

Oxford

MCO and its atmosphere suited Russell from the start (October 1908), and he soon settled down to the life of an Oxford theological student. Mortimer Rowe remembers him:

We were the best of friends from the beginning, and his friendship was indeed the outstanding fact of my third year at MCO ... We spent a great deal of our time together, including, I fear, much of the time we ought rather (by academic standards) to have been studying seriously and in solitude. Russell could tell a story remarkably well. When we foregathered, as we did almost nightly, round the fire in someone or other's room, many were the sittings to which Russell contributed much more than his share of the amusement or the interest ... [Remembering a walking holiday together in 1912 in Skye] I shall be there again someday I hope, and when I cross the Bealoch or scramble the summit of Sgun na Gillean, I shall be quiet and listen for some echo of Russell's voice.
(Letter to Lewis, November 1918 at HMC)

Russell made an equally great impact on **R. F. Rattray** when he arrived at MCO:

> *I need not try to describe him, he was arrestingly handsome, good looking: his dark eyes had great depths of tenderness and sparkled with fun, as he himself did. He was singularly endowed with gifts and graces. Everywhere he went he stirred men, women and children to enthusiasm about his charm and cleverness. There was hardly anything he couldn't do if he put himself to it. To Manchester College he gave a decided fillip – socially and academically. As editor of 'Poz' (short for 'Repository'), the College magazine. he made exceedingly clever contributions ... Russell had an heroic power.*
>
> (Letter to Lewis, 13 February 1918)

He was also highly successful as a student minister at Banbury. As **R. V. Holt**, another fellow student, recalled:

> *It was in the evening in his room that we used to discuss the universe. After some such meetings several of us drew up a statement of faith, and the actual wording was chiefly Russell's.*
>
> *– We believe in God, the substance of all things, the Spirit of our Spirits, and the ideal of our lives.*
>
> *– We believe that in the life and death of Jesus Christ is revealed most fully the self-sacrificing love of God.*
>
> *– We believe that Religion consists in the worship of God and the service of man in the spirit of Jesus Christ.*
>
> *– We believe that the service of man consists in the conflict with sin, the endeavour after social welfare, and the setting up of God's Kingdom among Men.*
>
> *– We believe in the Catholic Church of Christ.*
>
> (Letter to Lewis, 12 February 1918)

It is not therefore surprising that on leaving Oxford he was considered to be perhaps the brightest new entrant to the Unitarian ministry. The Principal, **J. Estlin Carpenter**, saw his impulse to the ministry as clear and strong (letter to Lewis, 6 March 1918), and clearly **L. P. Jacks** (letter to Lewis, 6 January 1919) was of a similar opinion. In 1910 Russell was appointed to serve as assistant to **Rev. J. Collins Odgers** at Ullet Road Church, Liverpool, and the world looked to be his oyster.

New pastures
All went well for a couple of years. Russell's success in leading the Sunday School was marked, but it is clear that he was restless in the ministry of a single church, however much his work was appreciated. No doubt to encourage him, he was made joint pastor with Odgers in 1912. He had met Elizabeth Durning Holt, to whom he was soon engaged; the correspondence suggests that she unsettled him even more, so that by the time of their marriage in 1913 he had resigned. The signs were clear in a letter to his former Baptist tutor, Dr Gibson, in July 1912.

I am afraid the different tendencies of the two pulpits is going to need some delicate handling. The dear old man [Odgers] is set on making everyone comfortable and nice and homely and smug and I'm rather set on getting things a little uncomfortable so as to avoid somnolence which is settling down like a cloud on us in the form of self-satisfaction as a Church.

Russell wanted a wider scene for his preaching, especially as his marriage had made him financially independent. In a letter to Lewis, who was at the time preparing to leave the Baptists, at Russell's prompting, to join the Unitarian ministry, he wrote (15 February 1913):

I've resigned my pastorate! I feel I'm simply impelled to do so for the sake of a work I'm simply bound to do; I'm boiling over with a gospel, and I find being in a church involves so much expenditure of time upon affairs to which I am not heartily devoted and which stand increasingly in the way of leisured thought and study essential to the work that I am set to

*do. So I'm offering myself to our Conference as a minister-at-large: I am
to go round whenever a man wants help in special efforts ... first probably
in Sunday services and subsequently, when there is a fruitful ground,
develop public meetings in some local hall – arranged by the local
church. This is my plan; and comes before Conference this spring: and I
have little doubt they will accept it.*

This was not to be, however, as the National Conference, following
detailed discussions with Russell, concluded that the Committee could
not 'take the responsibility of organising or giving official recognition of
such work without express directions from the Conference' (letter, James
Harwood to Lewis, 20 January 1918). He was deeply disappointed and
went around churches as a guest preacher for the next year, from the
base of a new family home at Presteign, Radnorshire. The advent of the
War could be said to have given him direction, as he had without doubt
lost his way.

To the end in Gaza
Russell joined the army at Liverpool as a Private within days of war being
declared. He visited Rattray, who had taken his ministerial place at Ullet
Road, immediately after enlisting. 'No one who knew Russell could doubt
his natural aversion from all that enlisting meant: but, as I have said,
anything he put himself to he could make a success of. He complained
bitterly to me how wrong it was that German wrong-doing should bring
upon people such sacrifices' (letter, Rattray to Lewis, 13 February 1918). L.
P. Jacks at Manchester College was in no doubt as to the rightness of his
action: 'I greatly honour you for joining the forces now fighting in reality
for Truth, Liberty and Religion. I envy you your youth. There is no doubt
whatever that you are doing your duty. God be with you. My three eldest
sons will join and I gladly give them to the good cause' (letter, Jacks to
Russell, 15 September 1914).

It is not necessary to describe here Russell's military career except in
brief outline. Within a few months he received a Commission in the 1st
Herefordshire Battalion. He fought in Suvla Bay in the Near East before
being invalided home for some months in 1916 with enteric disease. He

returned to serve in Palestine, where he was awarded the Military Cross at the first Battle of Gaza in April 1917. Russell then served for a time as a staff Captain, before being killed in action at the Second Battle of Gaza on 6 November 1917.

An obituary for him in *The Times* on 20 November 1917 was repeated in several newspapers, including *The Inquirer*, 24 November, which added: 'He was the first Unitarian minister who has been killed in action. He was a man of great personal charm and will be deeply mourned by a large circle of friends.' His letters to his wife are notable, and Lewis' extraction from them shows the great potential that was never to be fulfilled.

Walter Short

If the denominational press contains little information on Russell, the same cannot he said of Rev. Walter Short, Captain in the King's Own Yorkshire Light Infantry, who from the time of his enlistment in November 1915 wrote extensively on his army experiences in *The Inquirer* and *The Christian Life*. Following Short's death in action in France on 20 July 1918, **Rev. John Ellis** edited his letters home in a book, *Pictures from France*, published in Manchester in 1919.

While Russell came from a strong Baptist background, Short (born 31 May 1879) was in his youth a member of the United Methodist Church. He was one of many brothers in Sheffield, of whom four ultimately entered the Unitarian ministry: his brothers **Henry Fisher, James Horace**, and **Leonard** helped to found a 'dynasty' of Unitarian ministers. An ardent lay preacher, Walter left Methodism to join the Unitarians at Upper Chapel Sheffield. His obituary continues the story:

> In 1903 he entered the Unitarian Home Missionary College,
> bringing with him an ardent enthusiasm for the work of religion,
> every considerable capacity as a preacher and speaker, and a large
> experience of human nature gained in business life. His College
> career was eminently successful. He took many prizes and finally
> graduated BA. His first pastorate at Stalybridge (1909–12) was a

marked success, and he was called unanimously to Bootle in the Liverpool District, in 1912.

(*Inq*, 3 August 1918)

Thus Russell and Short were fellow ministers for a year in Liverpool and must have known each other. That is where the connection ends, although in 1912 both were seen as the best that the two very different Colleges could produce. If Russell made an uncertain way in the next couple of years, Short on the other hand was firm in his belief in his ministry of a specific church. His dissatisfaction, however, took a different form, as is shown in *The Inquirer* obituary:

> From the outset of the War, Mr. Short was deeply convinced of the unavoidable necessity for war and of the righteousness of Great Britain's entry into it. Everything in his spirit of ardent idealism led him to envisage the war as a mighty crusade for good against evil, a struggle for the holiest of life's values, in which there could be no other duty than to give all. As he understood the matter, the time had come when the preaching of the gospel could only be adequately carried through by deeds, even deeds of violence, and the injunction to sacrifice could only be enforced by unfaltering practical example. He felt he could not bid others go to the battle and himself remain at home.

Short's own words echo this evaluation at the conclusion of his last published letters from France (written 13 July 1918), after he had been at the Front for a long period, and his own Battalion had been almost wiped out:

> *Religion and War are strange bedfellows, but that soldier who has chivalry and idealism, achieves peace even in conflict, and enjoys the fruits of a good conscience, and the blessing of the Most High.*
> (*Inq* obituary)

His time in the army can be briefly described. After a year's training and waiting, he received a commission, going to France in January 1917 as a First Lieutenant. After experience in the trenches, he became a staff captain adjutant later that year. Returning to the Front in December 1917, he continued there until he was killed in an attack.

The army careers of both men were very similar, and even at home the 'dear old man' (Russell's name for Rev. J. E. Odgers) conducted both their memorial services. Each likewise left a wife and young son.

Evaluation

The attitudes of Russell and Short and their associates do not encapsulate the variety of Unitarian viewpoints on the War. Both supported it and saw Great Britain's actions as morally right, and there is every reason to suppose that this reflected the majority view within the movement. It clearly does so, if the columns of the denominational press in the period 1914–1918 are an accurate reflection of grassroots opinion. There was, however, also a very different side: there were Unitarian conscientious objectors and some supporters of the peace movement, although none of the former were Unitarian ministers at the time. Many of the ablest young men associated with Unitarians had been killed by 1918, which must have adversely affected the quality of the leadership among the laity in the 1920s and 1930s. However, the same cannot be said of the ministers who provided the spiritual and moral leadership. It could be argued that the Unitarian ministry had a 'good' war, if such a thing is possible, the examples of Russell and Short being edifying and up-beat. The service of several other Unitarian ministers in the ambulance service and with the YMCA was similarly positive, and they came back to serve their churches, often before the end of the War. It is therefore unlikely that they were the main conduits for the spread of pessimism that has been said to be one of the chief reasons for the numerical decline of Unitarianism in the 1920s. This indicates, as has been suggested, that the cause for the decline lies elsewhere.

Note

There are no accurate statistics recording the number of Unitarians in Great Britain from the 1890s onwards. The denominational press conducted censuses in the 1870s and 1880s which gave numbers for specific localities, but overall figures are difficult to estimate, especially as they included Sunday School scholars.The figure of 40,000 is a best estimate. *The Inquirer,* 3 and 10 December 1927, gives current membership figures for some 129 churches from which a national figure of 30,000 is a reasonable extrapolation.

Inq 1916, pp. 538–9, reporting a meeting of the B&FUA, provides the figure of 6,000 as enlisted, but over the following two years the numbers will have increased, mainly through the introduction of conscription that year. The B&FUA maintained a Central List of all Unitarians known to it who had been killed or died in the War (*Inq* 26 January 1918). The Supplement to *The Inquirer* 8 June 1918 consists of a Roll of Honour of 703 names of the fallen associated with churches and schools, relating to only one-third of the churches. The estimate of 1,000 dead is therefore conservative.

Among those fully accredited ministers who actively served in the War for varying periods were **H. D. Roberts** (Lieutenant 1915–19; born in 1858); **J. Cyril Flower; John Ellis; W. G. Price** (Royal Army Medical Corps, 1916–19); **Edgar Thackray; Harmon Taylor** (Captain RAMC 1917–19, who then left the ministry); **Evan Glyn Evans; Henry Gow; Charles Biggins; Charles Piper** (RAMC 1917–19); **William McMullen; Harry Andrew** (1916–20); **W. H. Drummond** (YMCA France, 1917–19, born in 1863); **F. W. Foat; L. J. Hines** (a Congregational Minister who joined the Unitarian roll following war service 1917–19); **A. S. Hurn; Lawrence Redfern;** and **C. P. Scott.** See *Inq* 1917, p. 104 et seq. (supplement): 'Some Ministers who are doing their bit', including photographs of Walter Short and T. P. Spedding.

Perhaps the most unusual example was **Percival Godding** who entered the ministry in 1912 at Ballyclare, Ireland. He volunteered for the army in 1917, aged 34, became a Lieutenant, and went out to France in April 1918. Taken prisoner, he later described his harrowing journey to a POW camp at Baden (*Inq* 29 December 1918, 11 January 1919). He is unique as the only Unitarian minister on active service to become a prisoner of war. On demobilisation he resumed his ministry at Ballyclare.

Sources

Manuscript material and letters held at Harris Manchester College.

The Inquirer December 1917, July and August 1918.

From *Transactions of the Unitarian Historical Society*, 1993

14 Rev. Sidney Spencer

Sidney Spencer (1888–1974) was a significant figure within the Unitarian community in the first half of the twentieth century. He was widely recognised for his pacifist views and their presentation during the 1930s and 1940s. In later life he was particularly known for his time as Principal of Manchester College Oxford (MCO) from 1951 to 1956, and for his knowledge and understanding of mysticism in world religions.

Spencer was born in 1888 in Nottingham, but details of his early life are sketchy. Originally destined for the Congregational ministry, he entered New College London in 1909, after obtaining a University of London BA degree in modern languages. He left New College in 1911 to continue his studies at MCO to prepare for the Unitarian ministry; he stayed for three years. On entry to MCO he wrote in his application: 'My parents are Wesleyan and I joined the Wesleyan Methodist Church at the age of fifteen. Within a year I decided to enter the ministry ... I became sympathetic with the New Theology movement when teaching at a private school in Nottingham (my native City) ... and had an early hero worship of R. J. Campbell. In 1907 I became a Congregationalist' (MCO Candidates' Testimonials, letter from Spencer, 8 May 1911). (Campbell was a Congregational minister in London, nationally known for initiating a radically new view of Jesus and the Christian ethic. Not a Unitarian, although many thought he was, he eventually entered the Anglican priesthood.)

At the start of World War I, Sidney Spencer began his ministerial career at the Free Christian Church, Narborough Road, Leicester; he served there for three years, followed by nearly four years at the Unitarian Church in Rotherham. Recognised early on as a good preacher, he first came to prominence during his ministry at St Mark's Church Edinburgh, which commenced in 1921. Here 'he began to make his mark as an outstanding preacher in full sympathy with the left wing traditions of St Mark's' (*Inq* obituary, 7 December 1974).

Perhaps the leading preacher among Unitarians during the early 1920s was **Rev. Dr Stanley A. Mellor**, minister at Hope Street Chapel

Liverpool, who preached to packed congregations. During World War I he consistently maintained a challenging attitude towards the government's war efforts. His sudden death in 1927 meant that the congregation sought to carry on this tradition with another noted preacher, and they chose Spencer. He found the task a daunting one, and before his appointment said that he would not envy the man who would follow Mellor. However, in retrospect **Rev. L. A. Garrard**, whose early ministry in the 1930s was in Liverpool, concluded: 'With Redfern at Ullet Road Church and Charles M. Wright at the Ancient Chapel Toxteth as his colleagues, he helped to make Unitarianism a real force in the life of Liverpool' (*Inq* obituary).

It was during the late 1920s and the 1930s that Spencer's pacifist stance, held since World War I, was regularly and strongly expressed, both in the pulpit and on public platforms. In later accounts of his ministry at this time there are references to 'disappointments', which no doubt relate at least in part to the opposition that he encountered to the expression of his pacifist views. Spencer was known as an intellectual, concerned with the world of the spirit, which may have made him appear remote to many. He supported the Unitarian Peace Fellowship and organisations working to prevent war in a difficult time.

Some saw his stands as dogmatic and often irrational. **Rev. Dr Arthur Long**, whose father was Secretary of the Peace Fellowship for a considerable period, had contact with Spencer over many years. He observed that 'Spencer was always shy and austere, a notably uncharismatic individual – and his eccentric manner of public speaking, with its rather strained tone and irrational heavy emphasis on individual words, didn't help. But what put many of us off – including those who supported his pacifist attitude – was the increasingly aggressive and intolerant way in which he presented his case' (letter to author, 2 February 2004, archived at HMC). Regular angry exchanges with his fellow minister **Rev. A. S. Hurn** of Great Meeting Leicester, who was an advocate of military action, did not make him a popular figure. However, he did motivate the Unitarian movement at its annual gathering in 1936 towards a peace-orientated, if not wholly pacifist, position. Spencer put forward a resolution, of which he was clearly the driving force, at the GA meetings held in May 1936. The text stated:

> ... convinced that all war is not only a crime against humanity
> but a colossal folly, and that peace can never be secured by arms,
> we, delegates and ministers of the General Assembly, definitely
> refuse to take part in or support war of any kind, as only under
> the sanctions of truth and love is it possible finally to establish
> right relations between peoples of the world. We therefore pledge
> ourselves to individual consecration in the building of world order
> on that basis.

According to *The Inquirer* (16 May 1936), 'The meeting accepted the Peace Fellowship resolution by what looked like at least a two-thirds majority. There was a call for a count, but the delegates, exhausted by the conflict, were already moving through the doors to the direction of tea.'

The following year Spencer brought the attention of Lancashire and Cheshire Unitarian Churches to what was happening in Spain. Another peace resolution was under discussion, and Spencer wanted an amendment. 'Here, said Mr Spencer, was this ghastly horror taking place in Spain, and the Christian Church stood in utter impotence. The churches could only make their influence effective if they took a stand on the ethic of Jesus. Surely the practical way was to give the world a lead in a bold and definite refusal to take part in this thing, to follow the method that said, "I will die for the cause but I will not take the life of another man"' (*Inq* 26 June 1937). He developed this theme in the Assembly Sermon that he delivered at the GA meetings on 19 April 1937: 'The call to religion, so far as it is of vital effect, must be a call to a Christian idealism which stands against the prevailing forces of the world – which stands uncompromisingly against the method of war, which stands against the struggle of nations and men for wealth and power that desolates the world' *(Inq* 24 April 1937).

New horizons

Spencer's second wife, Doris, writing in 1975 after his death, recalled:

When I first met him in Liverpool in 1927 he was as far from mysticism as anyone could be. His outlook was essentially political and social and he was wedded to pacifism and the Labour Party ... he had at one time either applied for, or considered applying for, membership of the Communist Party in Britain ... He was a natural student and as time went on at Hope Street Liverpool, his attitudes began, faintly at first, to change. In time he became less concerned with politics as such and more interested in something else ... he was profoundly interested in Blake's works ... and gradually came to see that the healing of the world could only come from the inward sense of the value of Love.
(*Inq* 2 August 1975).

This movement in his thinking came in the 1940s; but, even so, World War II tested his commitment to pacifism, which culminated in 1943 in his imprisonment: 'Rev Sidney Spencer is serving a sentence of one month's imprisonment for failure to register for fire-watching duties. Mr Spencer, who has been undertaking fire-watching duties voluntarily, considers it wrong to register for compulsory services in activities related to the war effort, even though they be activities he is prepared to undertake as a volunteer, and has twice refused to pay fines imposed' (*The Unitarian Monthly*, March 1943).

His congregation continued to support him, despite attention in the national press. Many saw his approach as doctrinaire in respect of an activity that he was undertaking voluntarily. 'This episode undoubtedly did much to alienate some of his fellow Unitarians, and he ceased to be regarded as a good advocate of the Christian Pacifist position' (letter, Arthur Long, 2004). In 1944 he preached on the subject 'Will This Be The Last War?', and he subsequently published the text of this sermon. His answer was No, because the war was just the repetition of an old disease, and a symptom of the real stupidity that he saw as existing in the minds of politicians. 'Mr Spencer may be dismissed as an idealist. He would not repudiate the description, but in his sermon he pleads that in the present world chaos idealism is the only effective realism' (*Unitarian Monthly*, July 1944).

With the end of the War, Spencer moved beyond pacifism and continued his study of mysticism in world religion. **Phillip Hewett**, later his student at MCO, remembers (letter to author, 5 November 2003, at HMC): 'He was very well-informed on world religions, particularly in their mystical aspects, but was evidently self-educated in this field, as appeared from his pronouncing Lao-tse as "Lay-O Tsee." This was certainly his main field of interest in later life, and I don't recall much emphasis on his earlier pacifism and radical social thinking.' Spencer now wrote quite often in the Unitarian press on mysticism and rarely on anything else apart from denominational concerns; pacifism seemingly no longer interested him.

He was involved in the governance of MCO and its associated institutions. 'For many years Spencer was one of what Raymond Holt used to call the Big Five of the Old Students' meetings (the others were R. F. Rattray, A. S. Hurn, William Carter and E. G. Lee) and was a prominent member of the College committee, strongly opposing any idea of a merger which might involve a move from Oxford. It was no surprise, therefore, when, after nearly a quarter of a century at Hope Street, he was appointed its Principal' (*Inq* obituary, 1974). It was, however, surprising for a non-academic in his sixties to be made Principal of a College which had hardly any students. His appointment was part of the denominational politics of the time, as the field from which an appointment in 1951 could be made was very limited. However, he was widely recognised within the Unitarian movement, despite his eccentricities, as a leading intellectual and someone with deep learning.

Principal of Manchester College Oxford

Whether Spencer can be judged as successful in his new role depends on one's vantage point. His students saw him more kindly than did the College Council, with which he had his difficulties, although he had formerly been one of their number. Spencer was not the first to be in this position, as tensions between the Council and the Principal had a long history: **L. P. Jacks**, for example, was in dispute for some years during and after his time as Principal.

First, the view of those who were his students. Phillip Hewett believes that 'he was appointed in the same way as John XXIII was appointed Pope, and likewise surprised everyone by doing more than temporarily filling the post. He did not impress one at first sight as being in good shape, but we discovered that he could play a mean game of tennis and more than made up in skill what he might have lacked in vigour ... I remember him as a gentle idealist who took the demands of his religion seriously and tried to live accordingly. At the same time he appeared to have done a good job administratively under the difficult conditions prevailing at the College at that time.'

Peter Godfrey recalls him 'as an extraordinarily conscientious principal ... If the College were to survive it needed a dedicated and hardworking principal. Sidney Spencer provided this. To a student Spencer's seriousness sometimes seemed to go a bit far. Not being allowed out of Oxford during term time was a bit irksome for a student who had just come from a redbrick university. On one occasion another student and myself were extremely keen to be in the House of Commons for a debate on capital punishment. We got out onto the London Road and began to hitch hike. Who should give us a lift but Sidney Spencer, driven by his wife ... Next day we were "on the carpet" in the Principal's office ... On a Sunday immediately after the end of one term I was booked to conduct services at Shrewsbury, so I left College on Friday. Next week I had a letter from Spencer asking why I had left college a day early and saying that the College Council would take a poor view of this matter ... Morning devotions were obligatory. A Swiss student missed one morning and tried to get round Spencer by speaking in German. Spencer gave him a full telling off in the same language ... The weekly coffee mornings in the Principal's house were always enjoyable ... Spencer cared for the students and there were several instances of his deep pastoral concern for non-theology as well as theology students. He also took very conscientiously his duties as preacher and minister to the chapel and its members. It is a pleasure to remember him with gratitude and affection' (letter to the author, 31 December 2003, now at HMC – as are other letters quoted in this article).

However, Arthur Long saw Spencer from a different vantage point. He served as a member of the College Council from June 1953 for the last two years of Spencer's time as Principal. 'It seems there were soon indications that he was not proving a very effective Principal. It is perhaps significant that my main recollections from this time centre round constant complaints and requests from his wife, which he doggedly brought before the Council and most of the complaints were trivial in the extreme ... (This) led to a most surprising incident which I remember very vividly ... Mrs Spencer was much exercised by the fact that inside the window ledge of an adjoining Holywell Street property was always untidily cluttered with packets of washing powder, etc. She wanted the Council to order the tenant to remove them "because people will think it is the Principal's window". We had asked Spencer to withdraw while we discussed what seemed to be some unreasonable requests. A long discussion followed, but the Council meeting was suddenly rudely interrupted when Spencer burst into the Senior Common Room where the meetings were usually held, and informed us, in what seemed an astonishing fit of fierce anger, that he was not going to wait any longer for a decision. I cannot remember how the situation was resolved!' (letter, Arthur Long to author 2004, and College Minutes).

In October 1955, in response to a letter from Spencer asking if his time as Principal would be extended, it was promptly decided that he would have to retire, as he was over the age of 65 (with reference to an earlier Committee decision on retirement age (College Committee, 6 October 1955)). Arthur Long recalls that Spencer strongly resisted this, on the grounds that he and his wife would have nowhere to live if his appointment was ended at the end of his five-year term on 30 September 1956. This was eventually resolved when the College Treasurer, Sir Felix Brunner, agreed to buy a house at his own expense, in a location chosen by the Spencers, which would be offered to them as a parting gift. The offer was accepted and they left at the end of the 1955–1956 session. 'It was a very sorry business, and Spencer ceased to have any prominence in Unitarian affairs, though he was appointed minister at Bath and Trowbridge, where he served for several years (1956–1970)' (letter, Arthur Long to author, 2004). No mention of this is to be found in the General Committee minutes.

Spencer took up his post at a most difficult time in the College's history, and relations with the College Council were bound to have been difficult. His wife Doris, whom he married in 1950, did not improve relationships with others then or later, and he seemed always to support what she said or claimed. He was not the first (nor indeed the last) Principal of the College to, in effect, be bought out to leave without argument. MCO could easily have closed in the early 1950s, and Spencer did keep the ship afloat and made possible the later notable Principalships of **L. A. Garrard** and **Harry Lismer Short**, on which the successful modern College is based. His regret was that he was not given any form of academic recognition, then or later, for his services.

A last effort

It came as something of a surprise to many when in 1963 Penguin Books published a substantial work by Spencer entitled *Mysticism in World Religion*. This book had significant sales, both in Britain and abroad, went to subsequent reprints, and was considered a standard work in its time. As Arthur Long (2004) pointed out, 'This would seem to indicate that while some Unitarians had always doubted his capabilities, he was probably seen in the outside academic world as an authority on Mysticism and Comparative Religion.' He wrote the article on this subject in an edition of the *Encyclopaedia Britannica*. Based on a course of Upton Lectures entitled 'God and Man in Mystical Religion', given at Oxford in 1950, *Mysticism in World Religion* was the second of his major works, the other being *The Deep Things of God* (London, 1955).

Sidney Spencer's achievements, if not ignored, were not fully recognised either inside the Unitarian movement or out of it. *Rev. W. R. Matthews, former Dean of St Paul's Cathedral, in response to a note from Spencer in 1970 congratulating him on the award of an honorary degree, wrote: 'You deserve the hon DD and D Litt far more than I' (Dean Matthews to Spencer, 18 July 1970). By the time of his death on 17 November 1974, Spencer was a forgotten figure, his deeply felt and expressed pacifism recalled by just a few people in Unitarianism and in Liverpool. If his name was associated with anything, it was for his painstaking and detailed study of mysticism. It can be claimed with some justice that Spencer was a notable pioneering contributor to modern thought, out of which arose the widespread interest in mysticism of later times.

Sources

Harris Manchester College, Testimonials, Council and General Committee minutes, letters.

The Inquirer May and August 1936, April, June August, and October 1937, November 1956, December 1974, August 1975.

Jacks, L. P., 1942, *Confessions of an Octagenarian*.

Personal letters to the author from Dr Phillip Hewett, Dr Peter Godfrey, Dr Arthur Long, now at HMC.

Publications by Sidney Spencer, including contributions to the *Hibbert Journal*.

The Unitarian March 1943, July 1944.

Who's Who in the Free Churches, 1951.

From *Transactions of the Unitarian Historical Society*, 2005

15 Raymond V. Holt at Unitarian College Manchester

The retirement of ***Herbert McLachlan** as Principal in 1944 saw Unitarian College Manchester at a low point. The Second World War had not concluded, and people's thoughts were elsewhere. In addition there was no obvious successor as Principal, and the College's finances, which had often been on a knife edge, had deteriorated. Whom to appoint? There were promising younger individuals who were not yet ready for the task. One canvassed name was that of **Lawrence Redfern**, the distinguished minister at Ullet Road Church Liverpool, who had taken an active part in the affairs of the College, and who was without doubt the favoured nominee of the retiring Principal.

However this was not to be, and the College governing body decided to appoint a well-known figure in the Unitarian movement who was about to become President of the GA: **Raymond Vincent Holt**. For over twenty years he had been Tutor in Christian History at Manchester College Oxford, where he had been educated, and he had produced some notable works concerning the Unitarian faith and its history. His *Unitarian Contribution to Social Progress in England* (Lindsey Press, 1938) remains a key, if indigestible, source book in this field. Holt had played a signal role in preparing the GA's Report, entitled *A Free Religious Faith*, published in 1945, which proved to be a groundbreaking work in the development of British Unitarian thinking in the second half of the twentieth century.

Few could doubt that Raymond Holt had experience in training ministerial students, but a key question is why he accepted the post. The prospects for the College were very uncertain in 1944, and it might be that a man aged almost 60 years could soon be out of a job. His father **Peter Holt** and brother **Felix Holt** were both ministers who had trained at the Home Missionary Board (the previous name of the College at its inception), and he himself had spent his childhood in Lancashire, but he had few other connections with the College. His half-brother **Professor Peter Holt**, from a different generation, who knew him as a boy and a young man, concludes that Raymond left Oxford for Manchester to satisfy an old ambition to have a college of his own: 'I believe also that he may have expected Manchester to be more congenial than the socially rather stuffy air of Oxford at that time for he and his wife Isabel were supporters of the Labour Party by conviction' (letter to the author, 2001).

Figure 12. MCO students in 1930, photographed with Rabindranath Tagore (in white). Far right, second row: Revd. Dr. L. P. Jacks (College Principal); next to him: Sarvepalli Radhakrishnan. R. V. Holt is on the far right of the main row.
(Harris Manchester College Oxford)

What did he set out to do? He made this clear in an address given at the Opening Proceedings on 15 October 1945. The text was published, and the principles presented in it are an excellent remit for a ministerial training college at any period:

An ideal Minister of Religion should be a person of deep faith with a high sense of a call to help others and an inexhaustible love of their fellow men ... a good preacher and if possible also good at business. He should be willing to work most of seven days a week and be prepared to face many discouragements and deprivations ... be good tempered and possess a sense of humour. If a student does not possess all these qualities when entering college, he is expected to possess them by when he leaves. And congregations are disappointed if this does not prove to be the case ... Colleges do not work miracles, and can only develop qualities already there ... if students are without this faith, with no sense of calling, if they do not care about their fellow men, then they ought not to be here at all. These are the essential qualities.

(*What a Theological College Can Teach its Students and What it Cannot*, Manchester, 1945, p.1)

In October 1945, at the conclusion of the War, Holt, supported by tutor **Lance Garrard**, had nine ministerial students, plus others in residence. In addition, he reported in his statement to the College Governors, 'every effort is being made to bring the College and Library buildings and heating systems into a thoroughly good state of repair and a valiant attack is being made on the garden' *(Inq,* 10 November 1945). Some of the students reported that the heating did not work at all well. In a time of fuel shortages, Hilton Birtles recalled that his room was the last on the top floor at Daisy Bank Road, so 'no gas got through to my fire for weeks'.

Money was very tight indeed, and **Ernest Penn** recalls that Holt worked on a low salary, as did other College staff, and made many economies, for example by building his own library shelving, using cardboard cartons and wooden crates. 'There was an atmosphere of informal domesticity ... I feel that some of his dedication and spirituality rubbed off on the students.'

Interviews for entry to the College were not the same as in the McLachlan period. **Eric Wild** remembers being summoned before the College committee along with **John Gill**. 'It was hardly a penetrating assessment of my suitability. I recall two questions, "How long had I been a Unitarian?" The reply was easy, "From Sunday School days." "Had I got a sweetheart?" The negative reply was easy because with my possible new future I had been dumped.' The setting for **Sydney Knight**'s interview was rather different: 'When I applied, Principal Holt asked to meet me in King Street Manchester. We met and made for the Reform Club, of which he was a member (naturally), only to recall when going up the steps that women were not allowed in and Margaret was with me! So the interview was held in the street – not easy especially as he was a good deal shorter than me. A further meeting was arranged in the vacation and when I got there, all was dark and silent and locked. I entered by climbing up to a first floor window and had a successful interview! I know of nobody else who has climbed into the Ministry thus.'

Holt had a distinctive style of lecturing. **John Storer** remembers that he lectured with a large ring-file in front of him. 'Each page bore just one or two words and the pages were flicked over rapidly as the lecture proceeded.' Eric Wild recalls that Holt lectured on Unitarian history and Christian Doctrine. 'Though these were the subjects he often soared brilliantly when like many academics his students ceased to exist. Lectures were sacrosanct, not to be interrupted under any circumstances.' Hilton Birtles found it rather baffling: 'The first page might have "God" written on it, then a number of blanks which he flicked over, talking all the time until he came to a piece with "Jesus" on it. By now he had changed his subject. It was all a confusing whirlwind.' There were morning prayers in the chapel, a recurrent theme of UCM life. Ernest Penn remembers: 'Everyone took turns at leading prayers, including the Principal, which took fifteen minutes and included a hymn'. Eric Wild recalls: 'We assembled outside the dining room in the evening and then went to hear a Latin grace. Naturally we were addressed as "Mister".'

The College must have been doing something right, as the number of students increased markedly, with ever less money to support them. In 1946/47 there were 13 (either full- or part-time, and including students for the lay pastorate), 16 in 1947/8, 18 in 1948/9 and 17 in 1950/51. By 1949 the College was running with a deficit of £1,800, and a Centenary Appeal was launched with the aim of achieving £10,000 by 1954. In November 1950 it had reached only £2,785 (*Inq*, 4 November 1950). The College needed income of £2,000 a year to carry out its task, a figure which was becoming increasingly difficult to achieve.

In 1949 Manchester College Oxford had few students, and the Council of that College concluded that it might be best to sell it and transfer the assets to UCM. This was rejected by a meeting of its Governors, and in its place was substituted a plan for increasing co-operation between the two Colleges with a view to eventual merger. In the meantime both were to continue to operate on their own sites. UCM wanted to go forward with any plan that would help to relieve its increasingly desperate financial situation (by October 1954 the Appeal Fund stood at £7,720). A liaison scheme was put in place, to be run by a joint committee with a ten-year remit. This continued for a few years but petered out in the 1950s and was not resurrected (*Inq*, 4 June 1949; 20 August 1949; 28 July 1951; 27 October 1951).

Holt did not take part in this controversy, at least in public, and unlike his predecessor his comments at opening and closing proceedings seemed to have been restricted to reporting the number of students and their individual progress. He was well supported from 1945 by Lance Garrard, who left in 1951 to become Tutor at MCO, and by **Fred Kenworthy**, a tower of strength, both as Tutor from 1947 and also as Secretary of the College. Experienced ministers came to instruct students in the practical ministry, for example on how to hold the baby at a baptism, using warmed water. Eric Wild reports his relief when **J. Harry Smith** came and talked about real situations that they might face as ministers: 'He not only made a great contribution to congregational and denominational Unitarianism but also to my ministerial education. I always felt that we should present him with some pipe tobacco, for he seemed to light match after match to ignite what was surely an empty pipe.'

Raymond Holt concentrated on his students and their activities. He was supportive in a way that was perhaps new. Students had been financially supported for decades by regularly conducting services at Unitarian churches in the area, which also provided good preaching experience. McLachlan often reported on the large number which had been conducted in a year, with demand sometimes exceeding supply. John Storer reports that Holt went further: 'He accompanied a very green student by tram on a foggy Sunday morning to take a service at Platt Unitarian Chapel. He sat in a front pew with an expression of approval on his face and sang lustily with each hymn. I was a raw and inexperienced student but on our way back to College he warmly complimented me on my performance.'

The students relished their Principal's idiosyncrasies of character. His writing was difficult to decipher, and it was claimed that when he had been minister at Edinburgh he sent a letter to a member of the congregation who, being unable to read it, took it to a chemist, who treated it as a prescription and dispensed it. This story echoed over succeeding generations of students, as did the fact that his wife Isabel had a broad Scottish accent, so that they were known as Holt and Haggis. A man of many interests, he transmitted his enthusiasm for them to most of his students, as was best summed up by **A. B. Downing**: 'He had too many irons in the fire and refused to concentrate … He was above all interested in ideas and in people. How vividly one remembers his interest in the Holiday Fellowship, the Fabian Society, Oxford City Council, in biology and birds and poetry – all this and much else besides, quite apart from his work as a scholar and tutor. He could play Gilbert and Sullivan on the piano and run socials and sing German songs. All these were as much part of him as his passion for social reform, his zest for liberty and reason and adventure in religion' (*Inq*, 30 March 1957).

Above all Holt was an optimist, and at the Opening Proceedings on 7 October 1954 he gave an address with the title 'I Am An Optimist: An Interpretation of Christian History'. On this occasion the College President, Lawrence Redfern, could not resist some naval metaphors: 'The good ship UCM was setting forth on another voyage at the beginning of its second century, with a pilot of the Holt line still at the helm and supported by his second in command Commander Kenworthy and although the crew of five students for the Unitarian ministry was smaller than usual there were good hopes that the next voyage in 1955 would see it increased' (*Inq*, 30 October 1954).

In this October 1954 address Raymond Holt summed up his philosophy, and what he had attempted to put over to others. 'He often thought himself to be the last surviving specimen of a nineteenth century optimist who believed with Tennyson that somehow good would be the final goal of ill ... He was an optimist because he was a Christian and also because he was an historian. Civilisation followed civilisation, but always something was handed down and not everything perished ... Today the challenge was that Society had become secular for the first time and the sense of the moral law had been lost. The danger was that the whole of mankind might be dragged down. Yet he could still be an optimist for again and again the life of mankind had been changed in one generation' (*ibid.*).

In 1955 Holt reached the age of 70 and it was time for him to retire. In his final report on the year's work on 5 July 1955 he went beyond merely telling of the good progress of the small number of students, although he confessed his regret that so often they made heavy weather of the Greek language (a deficiency experienced by many during their time at UCM, and not only under Holt). He concluded with a brief account of his stewardship: 'He found that of the ministers on the present General Assembly Ministers List, no less than one-third had been students of his, whether at Manchester College or at UCM. During his eleven years as Principal in Manchester he had supervised the training of thirty-five students ... Looking back over his time he knew that he could take away with him nothing but happy memories for he had met with nothing but absolute friendliness from his College and University colleagues, from the College committee and from all with whom he had collaborated in his various activities' (*Inq*, 23 July 1955).

A. B. Downing, in his fine obituary of Holt (*Inq*, 30 March 1957), summed up what was clearly the majority opinion of the ministerial aspirants whom he had guided through their time at UCM: 'Looking back, those of us who studied under him, walked and argued with him, are immeasurably grateful to have had some traffic with his mind and heart. Many an individual fire did he kindle in our spirits ... No image of him can grow vague or tired with time.'

From *Unitarian to the Core. Unitarian College Manchester 1854–2004*, edited by Leonard Smith, Manchester, 2004 (reprinted with permission)

---

16 Unitarian College Manchester: the Kenworthy period

Fred Kenworthy was the obvious successor to Raymond Holt as Principal of University College Manchester, and he was appointed in June 1955. He had been one of the star students of **Herbert McLachlan** (Principal from 1921 to 1944), whose mantle fell upon him. Born in 1909 and brought up at Mossley, Fred entered the College at an unusually early age and in a sense never left it. In acknowledging his debt to an early mentor, he wrote: 'I entered in 1924, still a schoolboy, qualified, but not old enough to enter the University. Fred Cottier [minister at Brookfield Church Gorton and a key figure at the College over decades] took me in hand. To a raw and nervous youth he gave much needed confidence but above all things a conviction of the supreme value of the work of the Christian ministry which has never left me' (*Inq*, 13 October 1973).

His qualifications to be Principal were impeccable. Apart from Manchester he had studied at the University of Strasbourg, held ministries at three Lancashire churches, and had been Tutor at the College since 1947. In addition he had served on numerous General Assembly committees and had chaired its Ministry Committee (*Inq*, 11 June 1955: profile). There was delight in many places at his appointment, as he was a man much liked and respected. His background in theology, biblical studies, and dissenting history was profound, and he was widely recognised as a quiet, kindly, understanding man.

In his Opening Address he echoed several aspects of his predecessor's declared aims, and it was clear that there would be few radical departures from the College's well-established principles: 'I am convinced that our form of free and undogmatic religion is a vital necessity in the world of today, and that unless we Unitarians present it to the world the case may well go by default ... The authority that attaches to our ministers has no supernatural source. It resides in the minister's sense of vocation, in his own qualities of mind and character and in the sincerity and thoroughness with which he has tried to equip himself for his work. The spirit and attitude essential to the devoted minister cannot be imparted by any college, which can only develop those that are there already' (*Inq*, 29 October 1955).

Fred was a shy man who found it difficult to converse. **Leonard Smith** recalls, in a comment which is echoed by other former students, that 'his silences could be an agony to bear. My mother never forgot the difficulty of entertaining him for a meal when he once exchanged pulpits with my father; talk was expected for politeness and Fred just didn't.' He was a somewhat sombre scholar, lacking in dynamic, but this deficiency was made up for by his wife **Ethel**, who soon became a power at the College and attended to its practical needs. In the view of **Bert Batchelor** it was she who kept the students in order. Together, in Leonard Smith's opinion, they made an excellent team, controlling things from their flat on an upper floor of the College.

Interviews for acceptance as a student were often brief affairs. **John Allerton** recalls that it seemed more nerve-wracking for Fred than for him. 'The conversation went something like: "Nah then, Mr Allerton, I gather you want to train for the ministry." "Yes" (Silence) "You're in the UYPL [Unitarian Young People's League]?" "Yes" (Silence) "And you went to Mill Hill [Chapel Leeds]?" "Yes" (Long silence) "Aye, well, all right then." End of interview. During the silences he made his very characteristic gesture of stroking the top of his nose with the crooked forefinger of his right hand. The students used to mimic this gesture, while intoning, "Aye, then."' Fred Kenworthy had a broad Lancashire/Cheshire accent which could on occasion be difficult to follow for those not native to the area.

The only occasions when Fred seemed to be voluble and relaxed, **Angus McCormick** remembers, was when sport, in particular football and cricket, was discussed. He was an avid supporter of Manchester City FC and the Lancashire Cricket Club, and their activities engaged his attention; he admitted that as a minister on visits to the sick, which he found difficult, he talked about sport. On a personal note, whenever I met him at committees and at other events I found little difficulty in engaging Fred in conversation, although clearly other Unitarians did. This was because we shared an enthusiasm for Unitarian history.

Fred Kenworthy did not spare himself in his 19 years as Principal. In 1956 there were but four students and a deficit of £829. In succeeding years the average number of ministerial students at the College was about ten. From a low base, financial conditions changed slowly for the better, so that by the 1970s the College was on a surer footing; much of this was due to the Kenworthys. A patient scholar, he always had time for his students, as well as holding many offices in the denomination, including the Presidency of the General Assembly from 1967 to 1968. **Peter Hewis** points out that Fred served on the Unitarian Faith and Action Commission, to which he made a valuable contribution. He contributed a chapter on Jesus and the Gospel to the book *Essays in Unitarian Theology* (1959), and while little of his work was published, his Essex Hall Lecture of 1958, *Ancient Prophecy and Modern Crisis,* is still worth reading. In addition he was joint editor of the *Diary of Richard Kay 1716–51,* published by the Chetham Society in 1968. However, as Leonard Smith remembers, 'there was always the anticipated book, which never materialised because of the pressures of simply keeping the College show on the road'.

The battle to improve the financial position was endless, as was the refurbishment of the College building. In 1960 a large parcel of the grounds in Daisy Bank Road was sold for the erection of a secondary modern school, enabling the old conservatory to be replaced by a common room, and extra study bedrooms were created. The following year external painting was carried out and new oil-fired boilers were obtained. These improvements were necessary if the College was to be successful as a University Hall of Residence for non-theological students. In 1972 dry rot was found, and yet another appeal was needed to correct that and to pay for more painting. Fred wore himself out in the service of the College and denominational interests and had to have periods of rest. Some believe that one of these episodes in 1959 was a nervous breakdown. **Rev. Ben Downing** briefly took over, but it was impossible to keep Fred away for long.

Everything was run on a shoe string. In the year ending 30 June 1966 it cost more than £10,000 to run the College, less than a fifth of which went on staff salaries and fees, despite there being a full-time Principal and three part-time Tutors. Domestic and maintenance expenses took up £7,300 (*Inq*, 8 October 1966). Fred and Ethel were often to be found during the vacations painting and repairing the building themselves.

The relatively high cost of domestic provision essentially meant food. It is said that an army marches on its stomach, but no less it would seem do ministerial students study and preach on theirs. Healthy young men, with strong appetites, living in College buildings not always heated very well, required plenteous food to keep them alert. The cost of feeding them was always a major consideration, which was particularly difficult when the College had few resources. It was not so bad when food was cheap in the 1930s. **Philip Tindall** recalls that while some students had the occasional moan about College food, he 'having been raised on good plain Yorkshire fare, could find no room for complaint. We had three good meals a day and afternoon tea, if we wished.'

However after 1945 the position changed: food prices were higher and College income low. But the College had its own vegetable garden, which helped. **Hilton Birtles** writes, 'There wasn't much food at College meals under the matron, Mrs E. M. Meldrum, who did her best. One dinner consisted of what looked like a mini-miniature burger about 1.5 inches in diameter. I picked up my fork, pierced this delicacy and popped it in my mouth with a flourish. One chew, it had gone and dinner was over. Raymond Holt said, "This is not a hotel Mr Birtles" but Ben Downing came to my aid and said, "It certainly is not: and if it were I should complain at the service."'

The position did not seem to change much when Ethel Kenworthy took over as housekeeper in 1956. **Tom Banham** recalls that she was the strong personality who pulled the College out of debt, although 'I did feel that cottage pie with an eighth of an inch of mince topped by two inches of mashed potato, and accompanied by more mashed potato was not that suitable for someone of my age.' John Allerton comments that the food was atrocious: 'Each year Ethel took great pride in reporting that she had managed to reduce yet again the College's catering budget. This was a time of considerable inflation! "Toad in the Cottage" and "Squeaky Meat Pie" were two of the favourites which we used to anticipate with dread.' **Allen Kirby** recalls that one Friday night when it came to him to say grace, 'the cook brought in a huge platter of dried-up slices of liver which looked like boot-soles. I took one look at this dreadful pile of leather and my grace was "For all thy OTHER gifts we give thee thanks, O Lord."' **Andrew Hill** remembers what he calls goldfish and polythene milk, which was a regular feature: 'Since I dislike evaporated milk all I ever had was the goldfish (tinned sliced peaches).' Andrew Hill and **Derek Smith** recall that Ethel used to sing at College functions, but we don't know whether or not she did this over the cooking.

One last food memory concerns the occasion when an attempt was made to change things. Peter Hewis was asked by the students to be the liaison with Ethel and ask for a greater variety of food. He contacted a local school catering officer who was a Unitarian, asking him to produce some interesting menus covering a month. 'The menus duly arrived and I presented them to Ethel, who took one quick look at them and immediately tore them up; on Sunday the students were still eating pork pie and baked beans as they had done for many years before.'

How did Fred lecture and teach? Leonard Smith found his scholarship thorough and sound, but he was never outwardly impressive. 'He lectured in his MA gown and would sit crouched over his notes, which he read word for word, but allowed space for questions at the end. But they were received with long silences and the answer came very slowly, if at all. He would purse his lips before speaking as if it was a great effort.' **David Doel** recalls, as do others, that Fred was believed to begin his Old Testament lectures each year 'by hunching his shoulders at the lectern and asking in a deep sombre voice, "Who were the Hebrews?"'

His tutorials could be different again. Tom Banham recalls those in Greek, from which he gained much encouragement 'of a rather strange sort. I would raise a question and he would stay silent with an occasional nod as, often in desperation at the silence, I prattled away suggesting possible answers. In retrospect I think he just preferred people to think for themselves. He was particularly good at the weekly sermon discussions and never said an unkind or unhelpful word. Mind you the other students could make up for that and he often had to act as a peacemaker.' David Doel adds that it was a pleasure to attend his lectures and seminars: 'I still retain good feelings about somebody who cared deeply and who was a brilliant academic.'

Like his predecessor he was tolerant of student excesses, both inside and outside the College. 'He did not approve of us loony lefties but, having made his views known, he nonetheless tolerated our distractions with politics' **(Graham Murphy)**. His own politics were Liberal, as distinct from Raymond Holt's socialism. Graham Murphy believes that he was the best teacher he could have had in those days: 'Who else could have greeted me with a wry comment and equanimity after having been detained, along with Peter Hain, by the police for disrupting the South African rugby tour. He confirmed me in a love of learning and of history, and although my first year in College was strange and unhappy, the succeeding three years under Fred Kenworthy I count as the happiest period of my youth.' Some thought that antics like never attending morning prayers through an inability to get up in the morning demanded action on his part. Fred did not protest either about the College float for University Rag Day. **Douglas Webster** remembers that these were noted to be 'the most hilarious and daring, one year there was a "Sex Changing Machine" when a ministerial student enlarged his chest with cushions and carried the slogan "Support Rag or Bust".'

There were other lecturers at the College to support the Principal. From 1959 **Arthur Long** tutored in Unitarian Thought and the Practical Work of the Ministry, and **Charles Bartlett** on Comparative Religion and Psychology, in addition to **Adelaide Trainor** on voice production. Bartlett was a challenging tutor in an area new to the curriculum. Douglas Webster remembers that 'he challenged us to interpret dreams his clients had experienced. I often responded, and my follow students nicknamed me Joseph after one session.' **John Midgley** became Tutor after Bartlett's death and **Kenneth Twinn, Joyce Hazlehurst, Stanley Whitehouse**, and **Eric Shirvell Price** were among other tutors and lecturers in this period.

Fred Kenworthy announced that his retirement would take place in mid-1974, but in March that year he died suddenly on the way to give a lecture. It was a time of flux at the College, as a new Principal had not yet been appointed, the proposals for a Manchester Theological Institute had just been made available, with long-term implications (Unitarian College eventually joined other Manchester training colleges in the Northern Federation for Training in Ministry at Luther King House in 1985), and the College curriculum was under review. The College Council decided to appoint Arthur Long as acting Principal until June 1975, when the position would be clearer (*Inq*, 6 July 1974).

While Fred was undemonstrative in all that he did, in conjunction with his wife he had achieved much. Peter Hewis recalls an 'Any Questions' panel at a social event held at Horwich Unitarian Chapel, when he was asked what luxury he would take to a desert island and 'his reply was, "My wife Ethel, because we complement each other".' Peter adds that his summary of Fred would be 'He had faith in us', and Andrew Hill observes that 'he was extraordinarily loyal and supportive to his students, whatever their intellectual calibre'. Graham Murphy concludes that he inspired remarkable affection: 'Who couldn't care for a man with such a pronounced stoop, and such a mangy-looking old dog at his heels?' **Ashley Hills** 'can picture him now opening the front door of Summerville on a rainy morning, soaking wet, and the dog shaking itself with vigour over everyone in the hall.' The final word is perhaps best left to Leonard Smith, a subsequent Principal: 'Fred's northern roots made it more likely that he would be most appreciated amongst those who shared them. I guess he is underestimated by the Unitarian movement generally, but there is not a student who will not testify to his remarkable influence upon them.'

From *Unitarian to the Core. Unitarian College Manchester 1854–2004*, edited by Leonard Smith, Manchester 2004. Reprinted with the permission of UCM.

17 *The Inquirer*: a denominational rag?

E. G. Lee (known to his friends as George) did not make many immediate changes to *The Inquirer* on becoming Editor in 1939. Perhaps the appearance of the occasional woodcut was the most pleasing development for the eye. There was little scope for much else, as the Second World War took effect on newspaper production; but whatever the circumstances, the periodical came out, which was a considerable achievement.

George Lee was a fine writer who, in the years that followed, had books published commercially, novels as well as works on religious and social topics. Some of his editorials are considered to be among the most inspiring and visionary ever to appear in the paper. Indeed, he believed that these writings were his best work. However, the complexity of his thinking was beyond many of his readers. As he grew older he increasingly came to be seen as an oracle; his personality and *The Inquirer*'s message became inextricably mixed in the minds of readers.

There were few changes in the presentation of the paper, except that short stories now appeared, and it was reduced in size as the years went by. It was during Lee's long editorship that the editorial office and business of the paper moved from Bream's Buildings, office premises in London, to become centred at Dr Williams's Library in Gordon Square, its printing by Headley Brothers almost a timeless and accepted ritual.

Like many of his predecessors, George Lee combined the editorship with the ministry of a London church, in his case at Brixton. The death of his wife and the need for a change led him to retire in 1962. Such a long period of settled calm could only mean that any successor seeking to bring in the changes that they saw as needed would necessarily encounter opposition from those who wanted to maintain a tried and tested formula.

Rev. A. B. Downing (known to most people as Ben) succeeded Lee as Editor at a time when the Unitarian movement was entering a period of internal turbulence, with new factions like the 62 Group wanting to ginger things up. Ben Downing, after experience in the RAF and the

Unitarian ministry, made changes in the paper's format, introducing new features and many more photographs. The alterations were obvious but not extensive, and they encountered strong opposition. The change in the banner heading of *The Inquirer* to white on a black background was a small point which annoyed many readers. A more mercurial and outwardly controversial character, less visionary than his predecessor, Ben Downing entered into the fray over the various disruptive issues within the Unitarian movement of the 1960s. In these circumstances it is not surprising that support for *The Inquirer* flagged, a position made worse by the death in office of the paper's business manager, **Percy Beasley**, in 1966. In the Editor's words, the latter was a 'tower of strength in the paper's often trying difficulties'.

By mid-1967, the fall in circulation and the worsening financial situation meant that the Board had to take some action. They decided that a new direction was required and accordingly they asked for the editor's resignation. Many believed that a closer and more direct connection with the General Assembly was necessary, especially as the GA's grant towards the maintenance of the paper was an increasing percentage of its cost. Ben Downing, whose editorship was imaginative and challenging, was caught in the turmoils created by succeeding a long-standing editor and responding to the internal dissensions within the Unitarianism of the time. In his concluding comments as Editor in September 1967, Ben Downing affirmed that he was carrying on a tradition: 'In general I am quite unrepentant about the sort of middle-brow liberal religious journal I have produced ... though it is apparent that many readers now see the need for something different.' In his last statement as Editor, he highlighted the tension that *The Inquirer* had experienced throughout its history: 'Unitarians are neither harmonious nor homogeneous. If they are true to their best tradition they can never be satisfied with a strictly "official" periodical.' The issue of whether *The Inquirer* should be a denominational news sheet had been simmering for some while. Some believed that it had served its purpose and should be replaced by something more uniquely Unitarian in content and thrust, and owned directly by the GA. The directors of *The Inquirer* Publishing Co. Ltd. decided to take a middle course: continue with the paper and seek a new editor, but move the editor's office and administration to Essex Hall to be alongside the GA.

In many ways late 1967 was a watershed in *The Inquirer*'s twentieth-century history. The periodical could easily have been discontinued and replaced by something very different. Its continued life is a tribute to the Board of Directors and their loyal supporters who decided to take it forward in difficult circumstances, as similarly their predecessors had done in the middle of the nineteenth century. The Board's patient effort, and endurance against a sea of trouble since *The Inquirer* was introduced in 1885, is worthy of record, especially the many years of quiet and persistent activity in the mid-twentieth century by its Chair, **Ronald P Jones**.

From *The Inquirer, A History and Other Reflections*, edited by Keith Gilley, Inquirer Publishing Co., 2002. Reprinted with permission.

18 Unitarians at coronations

The present Queen has been monarch since her father died on 6 February 1952, and her coronation in Westminster Abbey took place on 2 June 1953. We are having an extra bank holiday in June [2012] to mark her 60 years on the throne, and there will be special events. It is a long time ago, but I recall seeing the June 1953 coronation on television, as will some other readers.

A personal recollection intervenes here, because the week after the coronation the Queen reviewed the fleet, much larger then than now, off Portsmouth. My parents had taken me on holiday to the Isle of Wight, and on the day of the review I had to travel back to London for an interview for admission to grammar school, and there were few ferries. My father and I managed the journey successfully, but it was quite a task.

Figure 13. The coronation of George V, 1911
(Wikimedia Commons)

Wondering about the events this summer set me thinking about whether Unitarians were officially invited to coronations. The answer is yes, and I found the reference which set me looking at later events in the annual report of the British and Foreign Unitarian Association for 1912, confirmed in *The Inquirer* of 1 July 1912. Two representatives, the present and former Presidents of the Association, attended among the 8,000 present for the coronation of King George V and Queen Mary. The letter from the Earl Marshal instructed them to dress in the prescribed robes (hired, of course): 'one in court dress with sword by his side, the other in cassock and Geneva gown, and bands and scarf and shoes with silver buckles'.

Just one representative attended the coronation of King George VI and Queen Elizabeth in 1937, this time the President of the GA, **Dr N. Bishop Harman**, who described the experience in vivid terms in *The Inquirer* (21 May 1937). An interesting figure, he was a leading oculist, whose descendants include Harriet Harman, the deputy leader of the Labour Party, and Dame Antonia Fraser. 'Beside me was the Clerk of the Yearly Meeting of the Quakers, and Baptists, Congregationalists, Methodists and Presbyterians. The parsons were garbed in Geneva gowns and bands. The laymen were in court dress except for the Quaker who on account of his scruples was allowed to wear evening dress. I could not help chaffing him by an enquiry as to what George Fox would have thought of his trousers!'

It was roughly the same for the coronation of the present Queen, when the GA President **Rev. Herbert Crabtree** attended, but this time no court dress was required of the more ordinary attendees. But what was common to all of them, and the aspect on which each commented, was that they had to be at the Abbey to be let in by 6 am. There were hours to wait, and it makes me wonder what so many thousands did for toilets, as apparently when once inside you could not go out again. The report in *The Inquirer* (13 June 1953) was almost as vivid as the previous ones, Herbert Crabtree concluding that it was 'indescribable, I am so grateful that circumstances permitted me to see it'.

Nothing quite like this will happen in 2012, but I wonder whether Unitarians will be invited to the next coronation, whenever that may be. If so, the GA President that year will really have a bonus. The security arrangements will be stringent, as they were when my wife Rosemary and I attended the formal celebration in St Paul's Cathedral to mark the hundredth birthday of the Queen Mother in July 2000. We were at least allowed to go to the specially constructed toilets outside! Although we did not attend through a Unitarian connection, it was a notable occasion, not least because of the conversation I had with the person sitting beside me: Sir Henry Cooper, the former boxer. Only Herbert Crabtree mentioned the people whom he saw and spoke to, but that for me is really the main interest of these events. GA Presidents could tell much here of the people to whom they spoke at the reception held after the annual Festival of Remembrance in Whitehall. When I went in November 2002 I even exchanged a few words with Mrs Thatcher!

From *The Inquirer,* 18 February 2012.

19 Appreciations

Arthur Peacock (1905–1968)

Among Arthur Peacock's major achievements was the vital part that he played in the evolution of the Unitarian Social Service Department. Becoming its secretary in 1952, he was instrumental in creating a new feeling for social service in Unitarianism. He pioneered new ideas which had hitherto not been considered appropriate. His own experience in the Citizens Advice Bureau during the last war, and the subsequent social legislation of the Labour government, made him see that a new approach was needed in very different times. The church must become a partner of the state, and not its competitor, in helping any section of society in need; it was this role that Arthur Peacock tried to urge upon our churches.

During his 16 years of office, the amount of material, advice, and help for churches interested in social issues grew enormously. Contacts made by him in the wider world led to invitations to speak at meetings and were used as avenues for information and assistance. An excellent example of this activity concerns housing associations, where it was possible to get expert advice for churches who wanted to set up such bodies.

It can be said that Arthur Peacock brought Unitarianism back into contact with other mainstream churches in the realm of social responsibility, a contact that had gravely weakened in the period after the ecumenical conferences on social amelioration of the 1920s. He did pioneering work with the Churches' Council on Gambling and was closely associated with its administration for some years. The number of committees, conferences, and seminars that he attended on behalf of the Department was phenomenal, as was his written output. He never spared himself in serving our churches. In the Unitarian Leaflets series, 'Social Service in the Sixties', he wrote: 'But while the nature of social work may change, that which prompts Unitarian Social Service is the same – a concern for people, because people matter.' Arthur Peacock always lived this doctrine.

From *The Inquirer,* 5 October 1968

Note: Arthur Peacock's obituary in *The Times* (20 September 1968) was written by me. For a fuller treatment of his life, see *Who Was Who,* Vol. VI; and Alan Seaburg: 'Two Universalist Ministers: G. MacGregor-Reid and Arthur Peacock' (*TUHS* 2004).

Alastair Ross (1913–1992) and Stanley Kennett (1906–1992)

Both Alastair Ross and Stanley Kennett, whose obituaries have appeared in recent weeks, were experts in the procedure of meetings, and they gave freely of their valuable advice within Unitarianism. Alastair's knowledge arose out of his experience of the law, while Stanley's came from his sheer love of committees and meetings of every description. 'Kennett was one of the few people I have known who relished a committee and he was never satisfied until he became its chairman' (*The Independent,* 20 May 2002, obituary).

They were obvious choices for membership of the 'Group of Three', or in other words the steering committee which has become a regular part of our annual General Assembly meetings, since it was first set up in the early 1970s. I took Alastair's place when he retired from the task in 1977.

It can be said that Stanley towered over the annual meetings for decades when it came to points of procedure. Before the days of the steering committee, he invariably told the Chair loudly when he felt that a mistake had been made, and Stanley was, in technical terms, hardly ever wrong, He developed this role as the unofficial chair of the steering committee, and all that the other two of us could do was occasionally soften his sometimes inflexible rulings. When he retired from the steering committee, he still kept his eye on us and invariably told us when he thought we had made a mistake.

Stanley was one of the most clear-minded and technically knowledgeable procedural experts I have known. In the chaos that sometimes arose at GA meetings, he so often got us out of the mess of verbosity and lack of clarity (of our own creation) that seems to come like a virus on Unitarian gatherings from time to time.

From *The Inquirer*, 25 July 1992

Note: Obituaries of Stanley Kennett appeared in national newspapers, including *The Times* (with photo), which recorded the role that he played in the life of Liverpool over fifty years, in particular its musical tradition.

Magnus C. Ratter (1899–1993)

Magnus was the protégé of **Rev. J. Arthur Pearson**, for decades the London District Minister, who encouraged him to enter the Pioneer Preachers Hostel in the 1920s and later to train for the ministry at MCO. (The Hostel, in north London, was a form of Unitarian community of aspirant ministers, charged with spreading Unitarianism. It closed c. 1933.) It was Pearson's influence that had Magnus appointed to succeed him as District Minister of the London and South-East District Unitarian Assembly in 1946, in the teeth of considerable opposition. Magnus's feeling for Pearson is reflected in the obituary that he wrote in 1947:

> Long ago, when the world was to us very young, we came to Highbury (the Pioneer Preachers' Hostel): a Call had called us. The lively colts were frisky; with what shrewd wisdom JAP trained us to sensible snow ploughing ... He saw that we had an adequate dinner ... The state of the tablecloth and our learning of Greek, the trivial and important of our little lives, all was his concern ... He was our Counsellor... In our mature years it appears to us we learned more from him and from the hostel than from our tutors elsewhere.

From these few sentences we get a flavour of that unique style of writing that flowed from his pen. **Arthur Peacock**, who had known Magnus since the late 1920s, told me that he did not write in this idiosyncratic style at that time but adopted it in the mid-1930s. Epistles from Magnus were a delight, and I received several in the 1960s. One that I have retained and treasure concludes not with 'Yours sincerely' but with the following salutation: 'May the Alans increase and the Rustons multiply and converse'. He was an impossible but unforgettable figure who enriched our movement.

Incidentally he was a conscientious objector in World War I. J. W. Dyer wrote in 1970 on his own imprisonment in Dartmoor, 'The only Unitarian I encountered during those days was Magnus Ratter, who worked in the laundry, but this was before his Unitarian days' (personal letter to author).

From *The Inquirer*, 25 December 1993

Joyce Watkins (Smith) (1919–2002) and Trevor Watkins (1923–2002)

Readers will recall the obituary of Joyce Watkins in the issue of 18 May [2002]. Now, so soon afterwards, Trevor Watkins has died, on 20 August. They worked closely together and were seen by many as 'a team' committed to Unitarianism, so it is appropriate that this appreciation should cover them both.

They both came from long-established Unitarian families. Trevor was the son of **Rev. Matthew Watkins**, who died in 1933 while minister of Park Lane Chapel Wigan. His mother **Daisy** died a few years later, when Trevor was still in his teens, and for a while he lived with an aunt. Joyce was a daughter of the Smith family – and on her mother's side the Pooles – of Stoke Newington London, lifelong supporters of Newington Green Unitarian Chapel. Trevor, after war service, gained a degree in the physical sciences and was appointed a lecturer at South London Polytechnic, where he remained until he retired. He developed a deep interest in and knowledge of the history of Unitarianism, collected books in large numbers, and became a most valuable source of obscure information which aided many a researcher. Trevor's contribution to dissenting history was recognised when he was appointed to join the Dr Williams's Trustees in 1967. (Dr Williams's Trust maintains a library and research facilities in London, and individual Unitarians have played a major part in its administration since its foundation in the early eighteenth century.)

Joyce and Trevor met in the 1950s and married in 1959. It was from then that they became stalwarts of the Unitarian movement in numerous areas. At Newington Green they were ever present (with her father, **Robert Smith**, Joyce played a major role for decades at Newington Green). It was Trevor whom I met at the door when I first attended a service at 'the Green' in December 1960. I was not deterred, either then or later, so it can be correctly said that he played a real part in helping to make me into a Unitarian.

In the LDPA (London and South East Provincial Assembly) area there was hardly a time when they were not involved in one or other of its activities. They did not push themselves forward; both were quiet and unassuming, but their presence was felt in their practical service and commitment. When they moved to Worthing in about 1980, they became mainstays of the Unitarian fellowship there, and Trevor was still its treasurer until weeks before his death.

Those who regularly attend General Assembly meetings will recall that for years Joyce ran the bookstall with quiet efficiency, with help from Trevor, while at the same time she was also on the permanent staff at Essex Hall. Trevor prepared the distribution of the *Transactions of the Unitarian Historical Society*, even the 2002 edition, at a time when he had many cares. He also became President of the Unitarian College Manchester, attending the closing proceedings in June. Both were founder members of the Family Holiday Conference (an annual one-week gathering in August for education and social bonding) and they were among its key supporters at Great Hucklow (the Unitarian residential centre in Derbyshire).

Trevor was a keen cyclist and raised large sums for charity, particularly from those who sponsored him for his annual ride from London to Brighton. He started doing this in 1981, when he joined his daughter Cathy for the last part of the route. For the next 20 years he completed the ride, raising about £5,000 in sponsorship for the British Heart Foundation (see *Inq* 12 February 2000).

The list of their activities is too long to record here. In spite of increasing age they still quietly did more effective works for Unitarianism in a year than many achieve in a lifetime. Their deaths from cancer in St Barnabas Hospice in Worthing so soon after each other will be mourned by many, who will give thanks for two people who made a practical and positive contribution to so many things Unitarian.

From *The Inquirer*, 7 September 2002

Arthur Long (1920–2006)

I run a seminar for the Unitarian ministry students entitled 'The Unitarian Story in the Nineteenth and Twentieth Centuries' – not an easy task, as the period needs to be seen as a whole, and everyone has their own view of what has happened in the recent past. I've been doing this recently by giving the students a list of the most significant individuals: twenty ministers and ten lay people. Their significance is determined on a balance between their influence within Unitarianism and their status outside it. You could probably make up your own list.

Inclusion on my list is limited to those who are deceased. Few who have seen the list object to the names included, but nearly everyone wants to add or subtract entries. I will have to revise my listing now that Arthur Long has died. For the last fifty years at least he was at the forefront of our affairs – as a minister, speaker, author, college principal, and historian. His son Adrian has contributed an excellent factual obituary to *The Inquirer* (27 January 2007), but his father was such a leading figure that I feel that a wider appreciation of his contribution should be added.

Arthur played an active role in so many areas that it is impossible to list them all. For example, in the General Assembly, in the Manchester District (of Unitarian Churches), at Unitarian College Manchester (UCM) as well as at Manchester College Oxford (MCO), and in the MCO Old Students' Association, of which he was secretary for decades. He was a preacher much in demand, as illustrated not least by the Anniversary

Service Address that he gave in 1982 at the GA, when he reminded us of our origins. In demand as a speaker, he was always calm and to the point and witty; the latter quality he employed at amateur theatrical performances at many of our churches. If anyone bridged the supposed gap in communications between Manchester and London, it was he: he was born and brought up in Unitarianism and spent his early ministry in the latter and his active life in the former. His letters (and latterly e-mails) were a pleasure to receive, covering many subjects, events, and people, and marked by his erudition and depth of reading.

He played a signal role in the move from UCM's old home in Daisy Bank Road to the new Luther King House arrangement, which took place during his time as Principal. While this was the only course which was, in effect, open to the College, many felt at the time that it was a wrong move and inconsistent with our tradition. Arthur managed to persuade doubters where he could, and did much to assemble the votes in favour of the move. He played a key part at a crucial time in the College's history.

Arthur's loss will be widely felt. He was an elder statesman of Unitarianism, although modestly he did not see himself as such. His many students will no doubt recall the important contribution that he made to their future life and work.

From *The Inquirer,* 10 February 2007

H. John McLachlan (1909–2007)

John McLachlan, as the son of a historian of Unitarianism, told and retold the story of the movement all his active life. He was passionate about some topics: Joseph Priestley, for example. In an article that I sent him in the 1980s for inclusion in *Transactions of the Unitarian Historical Society* (which he edited for 18 years, exceeding the time spent by his father in the post), I dared to include some mild critical comment on an aspect of the work of the great man. I received a snorting letter back by return, asking how could I write such a thing, and declaring that he would not include my comment. I gave in and changed it, seeing that no other response was possible if the article was to be published. John had figures from the past that he saw as shining examples.

His output over the years was massive, and his work will be a legacy that scholars will use long into the future. However, his most significant historical achievement by far was his thesis for an Oxford PhD in 1950, published in 1951 by the Oxford University Press under the title *Socinianism in Seventeenth Century England*. From the start this was recognised as the authoritative work on the subject, and it remains so to this day. It is constantly cited as a reference in books on that period. At 350 pages, he wrote nothing before or after to touch it. It can be considered a masterpiece.

It was written no doubt with **Herbert McLachlan**, his awesome father, in mind. I once saw a letter written in about 1949 from Herbert to his son. He had gone through a draft of his thesis, pointing out a few minor supposed errors. He made it clear by his tone that John had slipped and needed to correct these at once. Probably all his life John had his own father in mind when he thought about what he had written, trying to judge what Herbert's reaction might be, and wondering if he would reach those high standards that his father constantly preached but did not always attain himself.

From *The Inquirer*, 24 February 2007

Dudley E. Richards (1911–2007)

This year has seen the passing of two significant influences on twentieth-century Unitarianism. John McLachlan's death in January at the age of 98 and now Dudley Richards's passing in Oxford aged 96 mark the conclusion of an era.

Dudley had a unique and remarkable style of conducting funeral services: he put his hand on the coffin and almost talked to the deceased. At the service for **Madge Hinkins**, who died at 95, he said that he had known her for over thirty years, but then he asked: 'What are thirty years in the understanding of such a long life?'. I could say the same of Dudley: for example, when I first encountered him at a service at Newington Green Unitarian Church in 1962, much of his signal work was already behind him.

Dudley was born and brought up in Liverpool in an Anglican family, but when they moved to a different part of the city they came into contact with Unitarianism at Ullet Road Church, then led by its remarkable minister **Lawrence Redfern**. He took this influence with him to Peterhouse College Cambridge in 1930. Here he stayed until 1936, perfecting his remarkable knowledge of Oriental languages. In 1935 he made his first contact with Manchester College Oxford, as a research student.

He became a schoolteacher, which was the occupation also of **Nancy Radcliffe**, whom he married in 1938; their solid family background, with their daughters, was to last for the rest of his life. Recognising that it was time to decide on the pattern for his future life, he decided to become a Unitarian minister and enrolled at Unitarian College Manchester in 1940. Events then did not go well. Dudley was always his own man and had his own view of authority, so he soon came into conflict with **Herbert McLachlan**, the martinet Principal who was nearing the end of his long reign. Obtaining a BD in just two years, Dudley was then thrown out, and nobody – including Essex Hall – was going to help him to become a minister.

His determination to minister, despite his financial problems, led Dudley to take lay charge of a unique independent congregation at Broadway Avenue, Bradford. Hardly well paid, he sought other income; for example, for a fee he wrote a Latin primer, which remained in print for decades. With a supportive congregation he created a remarkably successful ministry, particularly with younger people, over eleven years. So notable was it that he was finally granted ministerial status in 1947.

Times and attitudes changed, and he joined the staff of the General Assembly in 1953 as the head of the Religious Education and Youth Department. Over the next eleven years his influence spread nation-wide, and, with his guitar and singing, he made a signal impact on young Unitarians. The commitment of many to our churches over the next fifty years was fostered by Dudley at this time, and he became a well-loved figure.

A watershed came with a heart attack in the mid-1960s, when Dudley came very close to death. When he recovered, he decided to go to MCO to teach aspirant ministers and others. In the last three years before his retirement in 1977, he was also Vice Principal, a position that was a new and perhaps unexpected role for him.

He and Nancy lived at the College, at a house in Holywell Street, and their hospitality, both to individuals and to groups, became legendary. He created and fostered adherence to our faith through coffee and talk. I spent periods at the College in the 1960s researching Unitarian history, and I recall long walks around Oxford with Dudley late at night, talking about anything and everything, and this pattern was repeated with so many other visitors. Of course the discourse included Dudley's impossible question: 'What is a church?' Dudley knew nearly everyone, so the number of birth and marriage celebrations that he undertook was large. He was willing to travel anywhere if asked.

Dudley did have firm views, and the reasons for some of them were difficult to fathom. For example, he refused to accept honorary membership of the GA and would not budge even when it was pointed out that the award was not intended to raise him up, as he maintained, but was an expression of the affection in which he was held. As a Unitarian he was less than sure about those who held formal positions within Unitarianism. When I became Chair of the College Council at Oxford in 1986, I became aware of a subtle change in his attitude towards me.

Many believed that he should have produced books and articles, but that was not to be. He did preparatory work but always felt that it could be improved upon, so nothing resulted. However, Dudley's contribution was something different: he was above all a 'people person', and that was his gift. After his retirement he played a continuing role within the College and the Oxford congregation, ever supportive of the Principal and Chaplain. Frustrated by his declining health and inability to get about, he continued to sing and had the mental vigour of a much younger person. While knowledgeable about our history, he consistently looked to the future, adopting the words of Paul's Letter to the Romans: '*Be not conformed to the ways of this world, but be ye transformed by the renewing of your mind.'* This is a good summary of what he sought to achieve, and it is his lasting message to us all.

From *The Inquirer,* 17 November 2007

Keith Gilley (1936–2013)

Keith Gilley and I first met in early 1961 at Newington Green, where his parents were the caretakers. He was a young schoolmaster fairly fresh from Oxford, and not a Unitarian. I had just joined the congregation, and we had quite a few lively discussions, to say the least. Keith and I knocked sparks off each other, and we did this for decades. He strongly argued his case and, in contact with ministers like the **Rev. Gabor Kereki**, he slowly grew into Unitarianism. Keith left school-mastering to train for the ministry at Manchester College Oxford in 1967.

Figure 14. Keith Gilley
(General Assembly of Unitarian and Free Christian Churches)

Others will describe his unique ministry and the notable effect that it had. He was not a committee or organisation man – while that is what I have always been – so there were chasms between us; but we always managed to bridge them. The only time we grew apart was in the mid-1990s, when he felt that my support for changing the future status of MCO was entirely wrong. His emotional speech, passionately arguing that it should not become a College of the University, was widely respected, but his advocacy was not followed. However, Keith did not bear grudges, and we were soon on good terms again.

We stayed that way due to a mutual commitment to our chapels and churches. Readers may recall his regular feature entitled *Visitor for Worship*, where as *Inquirer* Editor he travelled round the country, attending Unitarian services, and wrote on what he had found. His evaluations, always kindly, were invariably perceptive and sometimes brilliant. ***Gertrude von Petzold**, the first recognised woman minister in Britain, was his heroine, and he became the recognised expert on her life. When I saw him last, he asked that I take away and lodge historic records that he held.

Keith was not a personality whom you would forget. He could be infuriating in his quiet intensity, but his sincerity and individuality took you with him. I was not alone in finding Keith to be someone with whom, on meeting again after a long gap, you could carry on the relationship as if you had spoken only yesterday. A remarkable figure.

From *The Inquirer* 16 March 2013

Index